HERBERT J. OYER

Chairman, Department of Speech
Director, Speech and Hearing Clinics
Michigan State University

AUDITORY COMMUNICATION FOR THE HARD OF HEARING

PRENTICE-HALL, INC., *Englewood Cliffs, New Jersey*

To My Wife

PRENTICE-HALL INTERNATIONAL, INC., *London*
PRENTICE-HALL OF AUSTRALIA, PTY., LTD., *Sydney*
PRENTICE-HALL OF CANADA, LTD., *Toronto*
PRENTICE-HALL OF INDIA (PRIVATE) LTD., *New Delhi*
PRENTICE-HALL OF JAPAN, INC., *Tokyo*

This book's purpose is to provide some structure to that area of aural rehabilitation referred to as "auditory training." It is recognized that auditory training is not apart from, but a part of, the entire process of aural habilitation or rehabilitation. In practice it is frequently combined with lipreading, speech rehabilitation, language learning, speech conservation, and the use of the hearing aid. Auditory training, as a vital part of the rehabilitative process of the hearing handicapped, deserves thorough examination and study.

Some basic principles that are pertinent to the "auditory training" process are examined for the reader. It is not the intent of this book to present a series of therapy plans, although some samples are included, but to discuss the training problems involved in assisting the hearing handicapped with auditory communication.

The book is intended to provide speech pathologists and/or audiologists in training and practice with relevant information that will hopefully make their encounters with the hearing handicapped more effective. Depending upon the training program, the materials presented in this text will be employed in courses labeled "auditory training," "lipreading," or "aural rehabilitation." It is hoped that this volume will also be useful as a reference source to psychologists, otologists, and special educators.

PREFACE

CONTENTS

1

AUDITORY TRAINING HAS OCCUPIED THE ATTENTION of educators and physicians interested in helping the acoustically handicapped for many centuries. As with lipreading, it had its beginnings in the early education of the deaf. Unlike the development of lipreading, in which well-defined and rather formal methods evolved, the development of auditory training has in most instances been generally less formal or structured.

In viewing the literature pertaining to this area, one finds that numerous writers have made many suggestions for training. A few of these suggestions are based on results of carefully controlled studies. More frequently, however, they are based on informal observations and experiences of teachers in training situations.

AUDITORY TRAINING: INTRODUCTORY COMMENTS

As one might expect, there has been a noticeable change in the general approach to auditory training with the development of electronic filters, amplifiers, and recording and playback equipment. However, despite the development of modern electronic training equipment and the advent of transistor hearing aids, the basic aim of auditory training remains essentially the same. In broad terms the aim of such training is to help the individual who is handicapped in hearing make better use of the residual hearing he possesses.

The audiogram in Figure 1 graphically portrays residual hearing of an acoustically handicapped child with a moderate-to-severe loss of hearing. The shaded area is the residual. The use a person makes of residual hearing depends on the amount of loss he sustains, his desire to remain in contact with the world of sound, and the auditory demands of his environment. Highly motivated persons often show tremendous gains in speech perception when given auditory training. In other words, a sharpening of skills in handling auditory stimuli often results from this teaching-learning process for one who is hard of hearing and interested in maximum usage of his potentials.

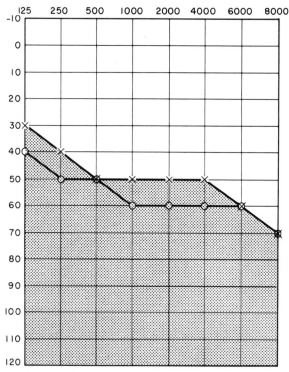

FIGURE 1. *Audiogram depicting a moderate-to-severe loss of hearing and the hearing residual. (Plotted according to 1951 ASA Standard) Key: X—left ear O—right ear*

In attempting to construct any definition, one risks omitting some important aspects of that which he attempts to define. However, we shall proceed with the assumption that auditory training can be defined operationally.

Goldstein[1] viewed auditory training as involving the stimulation or education of the hearing mechanism and its associated sense organs by sound vibration as applied either by voice or any sonorous instrument. It includes differentiation of pitch, rhythm, accent, volume, and inflection as well as analysis and synthesis of speech sounds presented as tactile impressions. His definition goes beyond the auditory input level to include the perception and integration of speech.

In his discussion of some possibilities of auditory training, Hudgins suggested that the possibilities include:

(a) The development of auditory speech perception
(b) Better speech, which includes greater intelligibility, more natural voices, and rhythmic speech
(c) A broader and more flexible language development
(d) Acceleration of the general education program as a result of improved communication skills[2]

Although not setting forth a definition per se, the implication is that auditory training is a special kind of training given to the acoustically handicapped that results in more effective speech perception and production, which in turn affects language development. This permits general educational acceleration.

In a handbook of exercises for auditory training, Kelly[3] suggested that he was presenting a plan of study leading to greater attention in listening, improved discrimination for the sounds of speech, and improved auditory memory span. He has implied that auditory training is a set of procedures aimed at helping the aurally handicapped become more proficient in attending to the sounds of speech, discriminating one from another, and effecting an increase in retention of sounds.

Carhart[4] in discussing the steps in auditory training makes the point

---

[1] Max Goldstein, *The Acoustic Method for the Training of the Deaf and Hard-of-Hearing Child* (St. Louis: Laryngoscope Press, 1939), p. 18.

[2] C. V. Hudgins, "Auditory Training: Its Possibilities and Limitations," *The Volta Review* (1954), 56: 1.

[3] J. C. Kelly, *Clinician's Handbook for Auditory Training,* (Dubuque, Iowa: Wm. C. Brown Company, 1953), p. iv.

[4] H. Davis and S. R. Silverman, *Hearing and Deafness* (New York: Holt, Rinehart and Winston, Inc., 1961), pp. 374–77.

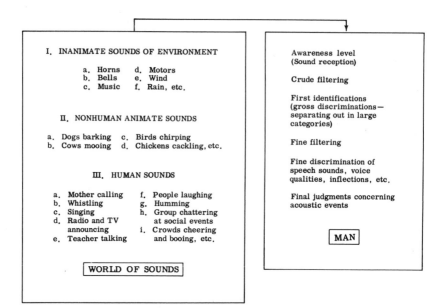

FIGURE 2. *Man's response to the world of sound.*

that auditory training is a process whereby the aurally handicapped learns to take advantage of all the acoustic cues still available to him. There must first be a development of awareness of sound, then training in differentiating gross sounds from each other. Following this there is drill in making broad discrimination among speech sounds, and finally, discrimination among sounds with highly similar acoustic characteristics. This outline suggests that the goal of auditory training is to alert an individual to sound and then help him to differentiate successfully all the sounds to which he has been alerted. Carhart suggests that a hearing aid cannot in many instances fully compensate for loss due to nerve deafness and that a course of auditory training is necessary. The necessity is increased if the loss has been present for a long time and the discrimination ability of the individual has deteriorated.

Heller[5] maintains that auditory training assists the person in becoming more alert to sounds about him and in discriminating sounds which are highly similar acoustically. A diagrammatic representation of man's response to sounds about him is given in Figure 2 and points up implications for auditory training.

When there is a deficit in the sensory system that causes distortions of sounds, there may never be perfect identification. The nature and severity

5 M. F. Heller, *Functional Otology* (New York: Springer Publishing Co., 1955), p. 205.

of the hearing loss, coupled with the individual's need to participate in the acoustic events around him, determine the extent to which successful response will be elicited by a training program.

NEED

In the first of a series of articles directed toward the training of residual hearing of the acoustically handicapped, Watson[6] indicates that in a survey of a school for the deaf in Scotland in 1891 Dr. Kerr Love of Glasgow determined that only 5 per cent of the pupils were totally deaf. A survey of 8,000 pupils in schools for the deaf made thirty-four years later in the United States showed that only 3 per cent were totally deaf.[7] In 1948 another survey in England of 353 children in schools for the deaf showed that only 3.4 per cent gave no response to acoustic stimulation.[8] The evidence from these surveys has encouraged the development of procedures for training the residual hearing possessed by acoustically handicapped persons.

The need for auditory training mainly arises with those who sustain hearing loss; however, such training is not solely confined to those who suffer a hearing handicap. Some people have no such loss, but appear defective in speech sound perception and production. Auditory training is vital for those who erroneously perceive sounds about them or for those who seem defective only in self-hearing.

Frequently, auditory training is needed for those who have been fitted with a hearing aid. It is also often indicated for those cases where the audiometric curve suggests that a hearing aid is not warranted because of normal hearing in the low frequencies and loss in the middle and high frequencies. In such cases auditory discrimination for speech is adversely affected.

Age is not a limiting factor where the need for auditory training exists. Successful work can be carried out with infants as well as with the geriatric population. The approaches, however, will vary with the age of the hard-of-hearing individual involved.

As with some other rehabilitative procedures, auditory training can be given individually or in groups. Successful training does not always depend on the use of expensive equipment, but may proceed if necessary with the simplest kinds of devices or without any equipment at all. Electronic

---

[6] Dr. Watson, "The Use of Residual Hearing in the Education of Deaf Children," *The Volta Review* (1961), 63:328–29.

[7] H. Best, *Deafness and Deaf in the United States* (New York: The Macmillan Company, 1943), p. 543.

[8] A. I. Goodman, "Residual Capacity to Hear in Pupils in Schools for the Deaf," *Journal of Otology and Laryngology* (1949), LXIII:578.

amplification and filtering devices, however, are extremely useful in controlling the presentation of materials.

The need for auditory training is particularly great for acoustically handicapped children in the speech readiness period. Lack of proper attention during this time can result not only in articulatory difficulties but also in basic problems of language development and scholastic achievement. An accurate generalization is that auditory training is needed by all those having difficulty in the perception of speech.

SCOPE OF THE TEXT

The next chapter of this text will be devoted to a discussion of the historical development of auditory training.

The following two chapters will consider the problems associated with hearing loss and the perceptual organization of auditory events.

Chapters 5 and 6 concern the factors that are important to consider when giving auditory training and the effects of auditory training upon the development of language.

Available equipment that can be useful in auditory training is discussed in Chapter 7.

The importance of listening is emphasized in Chapter 8.

Since auditory training can be given individually or in groups, care has been taken to outline the advantages and limitations of both approaches in Chapters 9 and 10.

Because a program of aural rehabilitation frequently embraces lipreading and speech therapy, the necessity for combined approaches is treated in Chapter 11.

A review of printed and recorded materials followed by an analysis and evaluation of these materials is made in Chapter 12.

Since hearing loss is frequently a contributing factor in those handicapped by other conditions, suggestions are made for auditory training of the multiply handicapped in Chapter 13.

Chapter 14 is directed toward the measurement of success in programs of auditory training. A limited amount of well-controlled research which deals with the effects of auditory training has been done. This dearth of research is not peculiar to the area of auditory training but characterizes other areas of speech and hearing rehabilitation.

SUMMARY

In this chapter there are brief remarks that introduce the area of auditory training, which is one of the approaches used in habilitation and rehabilitation of the hearing-handicapped individual. The concept of residual hearing, which comprises the focal point in auditory training, has been set forth. Operational definitions of auditory training have been given. Also the need for specialized training in audition by those who sustain loss of hearing has been emphasized. The last section outlined the scope of this text.

2

THE IMPORTANCE OF AUDITORY TRAINING IN THE
habilitation or rehabilitation of acoustically handicapped persons was recognized centuries ago.
Then, as today, the emphasis was on stimulating
the hearing mechanism, thereby enabling use of
the residual hearing.

BEFORE 1900

Goldstein[1] points out that as early as the first
century Archigenes suggested that a hearing trumpet and loud sounds be used in the cases of the

[1] Max Goldstein, *The Acoustic Method for the Training of the
Deaf and Hard-of-Hearing Child* (St. Louis: Laryngoscope Press,
1939), p. 11.

HISTORICAL
PERSPECTIVE

hard of hearing. Five centuries later, Alexander of Tralles[2] advocated that various kinds of noises and shouting be employed to stimulate the hearing function of those who were auditorally handicapped. Approximately one thousand years later the same notion was emphasized by Guido Guidi.

In the eighteenth century, when society not only recognized the need but assumed the responsibility for the education of the aurally handicapped, much more emphasis was placed on speech training. With efforts directed toward speech and language development, the study of auditory training and lipreading was given much consideration. At this time hand signals and fingerspelling were also emphasized by some educators.

In 1761 Ernaud[3] showed the Academy of Sciences in Paris that acoustically handicapped persons with some residual hearing could develop, through exercise, auditory discrimination for words and phrases. A few years later Pereire, a teacher of the deaf, suggested that nearly all deaf pupils who had some remnant of hearing could be trained to hear and understand some speech.

Early in the nineteenth century (1802), a French physician named Itard[4] demonstrated that auditory training had real value for the hard of hearing. Working with a group of six pupils who had been classified as deaf, Itard used bells to stimulate their residual hearing. As they perceived the presence of the sound made by the ringing of the bells, he gradually reduced the intensity. He moved from the use of bells to musical tones, drum beats, flute notes, sustained vowel sounds, and consonants. The ability to hear and understand words was developed in two of the six cases after a year of practice.

Itard's work became known to others who were concerned with the problem of educating the deaf. His methods, or at least a modification of them, were subsequently used in other training centers. Probably the most important contribution made by Itard in the area of auditory training was his use of different kinds of sound producing sources and his systematic employment of them over a prolonged period.

He died in 1832, but his ideas for auditory training of hearing-handicapped persons survived. Blanchet and Deleau used his methods in France. Beck, Jager, and Wolff employed his approach in Germany.

Thirty years later in England, an educator of the deaf named Toynbee supported the ideas of Itard that were relative to auditory stimulation. Toynbee reasoned that if Itard's notions about the amount of residual hearing among those classified as deaf were true, approximately only 50 per cent of those in deaf schools were really deaf. He emphasized the necessity for training that would help the acoustically handicapped learn

2 *Ibid.*, p. 11.
3 *Ibid.*, p. 11.
4 *Ibid.*, p. 11.

to develop better control over their voices. Much of the training was with amplified language units, that is, sounds, words, phrases, and sentences.

In Vienna, Urbantschitsch[5] carried out some experimentation in auditory training with persons classified as deaf. In 1893 he demonstrated his work with eighteen students and showed how these subjects, who did not respond to hearing tests before training, could differentiate language units ranging from vowels to entire sentences after auditory training. Goldstein learned of the work of Urbantschitsch and employed his method at the St. Joseph School for the Deaf. In 1897 he demonstrated the method with students before the American Academy of Ophthalmology and Otolaryngology.

Before 1900 auditory training was given in the Nebraska School for the Deaf. One instructor reported in 1893 that after a month of training his class was able to speak, hear or lipread, and write sentences.

AFTER 1900

A few years after Central Institute for the Deaf was founded in St. Louis (1914), Goldstein incorporated his Acoustic Method as a separate and distinct approach in teaching the deaf and probably made a greater contribution to auditory training than any of his American contemporaries. Interest in helping the deaf utilize their residual hearing spread to other institutions. Methods employed were variously referred to as acoustic training, auditory training, and auricular training. The interest shown by influential persons such as A. G. Bell, John Clarke, and Thomas Gallaudet helped immeasurably to popularize the idea that many who had been considered deaf could be helped by aural stimulation. Bell suggested the first group auditory training unit when he urged the deaf pupils be given telephones connected directly to a teacher's telephone.

Until people were trained as audiologists, interest in auditory training was largely manifested by teachers in schools for the deaf or instructors in training programs preparing teachers of the deaf. As Hudgins[6] points out, the interest and enthusiasm for auditory training shown by schools for the deaf varied from time to time depending upon the success achieved by the pupils. Continued effort in auditory training was not expended by deaf schools as a whole until electronic amplifying devices were made available in the 1920's. With their advent, new interest was manifested in the training of residual hearing. Group training units have been in-

---

[5] *Ibid.,* p. 15.

[6] C. V. Hudgins, "Auditory Training: Its Possibilities and Limitations," *The Volta Review* (1954), 56:339.

stalled in many schools, and those children having some residual hearing have been given educational instruction under headphones.

Following World War II, professional workers became engaged in aural rehabilitation of veterans who had become hard of hearing during military service. Audiology centers were established at the Deshon, Borden, and Hoff General Hospitals for the United States Army. The United States Naval Hospital in Philadelphia also set up an audiology clinic. Anderman[7] judges that the military programs provided hearing rehabilitative service to approximately 15,000 veterans. He estimates that today 56,000 veterans of World War II have service-connected hearing impairment or ear disease. In addition there are 24,000 veterans other than those of World War II who need audiological service. Some of these veterans have been and are being seen on an inpatient basis; however, the majority receive help as outpatients in VA Centers or in the VA contract clinics throughout the country. Auditory training has been an integral part of the hearing rehabilitation services rendered the veterans. Some may receive training when no hearing aid is prescribed, whereas others may receive it after being fitted with an aid.

An important fact is made evident in the VA programs, namely that the federal government recognizes the importance of auditory training as a part of aural rehabilitation and is willing to underwrite the cost of this training for men and women who have become hearing handicapped during military service.

Soon after World War II, the Army hospitals were closed. Johnson[8] implies that professional service rendered the hearing handicapped became better known to the general public because the veterans were then treated in privately and publicly supported university clinics, hospitals, and other centers. Today there are 166 hearing service centers in the United States, according to the Downs[9] survey. The percentage of those centers reporting that they provide auditory training is as follows:

	Per cent
University	100
Medical school or hospital	83.3
Hearing societies	100
Federal agencies	82.2
State agencies	60.0
Public agencies	88.9
Private agencies	100

[7] H. Davis and S. R. Silverman, *Hearing and Deafness,* rev. ed. (New York: Holt, Rinehart and Winston, Inc., 1960), p. 477.

[8] K. O. Johnson, "Audiology Progress and Problems," *A.M.A. Archives of Otolaryngology* (1961), 73:381.

[9] Marion Downs, "Hearing Rehabilitation Centers in the United States," *A.M.A. Archives of Otolaryngology* (1961), 73:65–89.

These figures show the great emphasis that is being placed on helping the acoustically handicapped make better use of residual hearing. In some colleges and universities, auditory training is taught to speech and hearing clinicians as a course apart from other rehabilitative procedures. In other institutions it is combined with lipreading.

A great amount of research has been carried out in the field of audition, but a real need exists for research that is aimed at measuring the effectiveness of auditory training methods as they are applied to the hard of hearing. As with the teaching of lipreading, there are manuals available that present training materials. These materials will be considered in Chapter 12. Perhaps one day a standardized approach based on experimental research results will be available.

SUMMARY

Auditory training is not of recent origin but was employed centuries ago by some who were interested in helping acoustically handicapped individuals. Although the methods employed were crude, the results obtained were promising. Through stimulation of the auditory mechanisms, it was found that many who had been classified as deaf were really not profoundly deaf but hard of hearing, and had a residual of hearing that could be useful if trained.

Schools for the deaf were the first to offer auditory training, but with the advent of the discipline of audiology, such training has become an integral part of the aural rehabilitation programs in hospitals, universities, and hearing centers located in other environments. Theory and methods in auditory training comprise a part of the course work taken by students preparing for careers in hearing therapy and also by those preparing for education of the deaf.

There have been a few specific procedures suggested for auditory training by persons working with the hearing handicapped. In some instances these procedures have been published in manuals, handbooks, and other media for use in training situations. As yet, however, there is a great need for research on the effects of auditory training. With research data at hand, perhaps a more scientific approach could be made to this area of aural rehabilitation.

3

THE TITLE OF THIS CHAPTER IMPLIES THAT HEAR-
ing loss creates problems that must be dealt with
by persons sustaining such loss. It is not always
true, however, that those who have a loss of hearing have pressing problems to solve. Certainly the
number, type, and magnitude of the problems associated with hearing loss are a function of several
factors, among which are the nature and severity
of the hearing loss, time of onset of the loss, the
extent of habilitative or rehabilitative measures
undertaken, the reaction of the person toward his
loss, the reaction of others toward the loss, and
so forth. Since no two persons are the same, one
could expect that the problems encountered by any
two persons with highly similar case histories might

PROBLEMS
ASSOCIATED
WITH HEARING LOSS

be quite different. Despite the fact that behavior might vary greatly between any two persons with similar histories and loss patterns, there are some general areas of concern to which the clinician engaged in aural rehabilitation directs his attention when dealing with the child or adult suffering from loss of hearing.

ASSESSMENT OF HEARING HANDICAP

To determine the nature and severity of a hearing loss calls for audiometric measurement, but to determine the handicap that results from the loss is quite another matter. Therefore, one should view the labels *hearing loss* and *hearing handicap* as two distinctly different things. Much energy has been expended by audiologists in the construction of tests to determine how well or how poorly a person hears pure tones and speech. Great strides have been made in the development of testing procedures that help to specify the site of the lesion. Tests have been constructed that allow one to determine whether or not the hearing loss is an organic or functional one. Other tests provide rather objective measurement of hearing without requiring overt response from the person being tested. Indeed, information regarding the measurement of hearing level is still incomplete, but it is possible at present to describe with some precision the status of one's hearing.

Very few generalizations can be made, on the basis of scientific evidence, about the amount of handicap that may result from hearing loss. To one engaged in pursuits that entail constant contact with people, a slight-to-moderate loss of hearing might prove quite handicapping, whereas to another whose daily routines have little if anything to do with communicating with others, this same degree of loss might be almost unnoticed. In other words, there is not a one-to-one relationship between *hearing loss* and *hearing handicap*, but rather the *hearing handicap* varies as a function of the demands that are placed on the person with the loss. Thus, it behooves the clinician to evaluate the need for auditory training for any one individual on the basis of the hearing handicap that is presented.

There are several areas that the clinician will wish to explore and likewise several methods of exploration he might employ. The areas suggested here are not in any sense mutually exclusive. On the contrary, there is great overlap among them. The broad areas in which handicaps are frequently noted when hearing loss is present are (1) communication, (2) self-adjustment, (3) social adjustment, (4) school achievement, and (5) vocational adjustment.

COMMUNICATION

One of the areas in which hearing handicap occurs is that of communication. Even though a great deal of human communication is nonverbal in character, success in many daily situations depends on one's ability to receive and sort out acoustic stimuli, some of which are units of language. If the system that receives and sorts is faulty one can expect that errors will occur. However, if sufficient visual stimuli supply information that is missed because of a faulty auditory mechanism, the person who is hearing handicapped will receive the message.

As one views the human communication process, he realizes that for communication to occur there must be an origin of that which is to be communicated—a *source*. That which is to be communicated is commonly referred to as the *code*. The component that sends forth the code is the *transmitter*. As the code is sent forth, it is sent through a *channel* or perhaps several channels. At the terminal point in the channel, it is picked up by a *receiver*. Following message reception, a process occurs wherein the code is perceived and serves to evoke meanings. If, anywhere along the line, the communication process fails, then errors can occur. Errors can be highly significant or of little importance, depending on the relative importance of the message to the source or to the receiver. Thus, as one scrutinizes more carefully the components of the communication system and attempts to relate hearing loss to that system's functioning, certain observations and generalizations can be made which may create a better understanding of the communication problems associated with hearing loss.

SOURCE

Since communication involves the sending of information, one concludes rather quickly that the information to be sent must reside somewhere. For the human communication system, information is stored within the cerebrum. It is important to determine what effect hearing loss can have on information that is to be transmitted. If this information has been acquired through a receiving system that is malfunctioning due to hearing loss, then the stored information may be distorted and invalid. The hearing loss could affect the credibility of the source. However, it is hard to judge the extent to which this handicaps the person suffering the loss or other people who could be affected by faulty information he might transmit. It would be very difficult to measure the amount of misunderstanding resulting from the transmission of erroneous information by a single person, to say nothing of the entire population of the hard of hearing. If an accurate measure of the misunderstanding could be made, it would be even more impossible to attempt to assess the actual handicaps that occurred.

CODE

The vehicle that carries information to a receiver is known as the code. When people communicate with one another, the code consists of oral or written language units and/or bodily gestures or postures. In other words, the code consists of auditory or visual signals that convey information that makes sense to the perceiver as it evokes meanings. In the strict sense, one could say that loss of hearing, per se, has no effect on the code. However, it might well be argued that the skill with which the code is employed could most certainly be affected by hearing loss, because concept formation and vocabulary development are greatly enhanced by learning that is associated with auditory experiences.

TRANSMITTER

Hearing loss has no adverse effect on the structure of the transmitter; however, it can have serious effects on the functioning of the transmitting mechanism. The malfunction is not caused by organic problems relating to the development of the voice and articulation systems in the transmitting mechanism, but rather by problems associated with learning how the mechanism must function to handle the code acceptably. Teaching children born with severe auditory defects to speak becomes a matter of great concern. Helping those who suffer hearing loss after learning oral language, to conserve good voice and articulation is often a problem. Hence, hearing loss can be of tremendous importance in the functioning of the transmitter because of the restriction it may impose upon the receiver as a monitoring mechanism.

CHANNEL

The medium through which information is sent is referred to as the channel. This might be the air between speaker and listener, telephone wires, radio waves, and so on. The efficiency of a channel is in part a function of its capacity, that is the amount of information that can be conveyed through it. Its efficiency is also attributable to the freedom that exists within the channel from competing irrelevant signals. Although hearing loss can have profound effects on the events at both ends of the channel, it would be difficult to attribute inadequacy of channel function to auditory deficit.

RECEIVER

Hearing loss can have profound effects on receiver performance. Errors in communication tend to increase with the increase in severity of hearing loss. A logical question arises concerning the manner in which errors occur in relation to the nature and severity of the hearing loss. Certainly one would expect a relationship to exist between the acoustic composition of auditory language signals and the efficiency of the receiver as related to the nature of the hearing loss. That is, if one could not hear the high-frequency sounds well, it would follow that those speech sounds having high-frequency characteristics would probably be misunderstood. The whole picture is complicated by the fact that speech sounds do not just neatly drop out as one sustains a loss at certain frequencies, but rather they become distorted. If the distortion is great enough to alter substantially the information the receiver gets, one could expect that a real handicap might attend the loss. But, once more, the extent of the handicap would be an individual matter, depending on the individual need for a receiver mechanism that functioned well.

It is accepted as fact that babies learn to talk because they hear themselves and hear others about them. With a receiving system that is operating inadequately, or not at all, one can expect that speech and language will be adversely affected. Probably the greatest handicap in communication occurs when the receiver does not function at all or functions poorly at the baby's birth or before he has learned to make sense of the multitude of different acoustic events with which he is bombarded.

Figure 3 shows the frequency and intensity characteristics of most of the fundamental sounds of speech.[1] In the original figure by Fletcher, the sounds were represented with diacritical markings but in Figure 3 they have been translated to phonetic characters. From the information provided in Figure 3 one begins to get some notion about hearing loss and its possible effects on speech sound reception and discrimination.

More precise information about receiver malfunction can be gained through the administration of standardized tests of speech reception. A test that is useful with older children and adults is the C.I.D. Auditory Test W-1. It is composed of words with spondaic stress pattern and is extremely helpful in determining a speech reception threshold. In order to assess auditory discrimination performance, another group of standardized test lists are employed. They are phonetically balanced; hence they are called the PB's—formally referred to as the C.I.D. Auditory

---

[1] H. Fletcher, *Speech and Hearing in Communication,* Bell Telephone Laboratories, Inc. (Princeton, N.J.: D. Van Nostrand Co. Inc., 1953), p. 87.

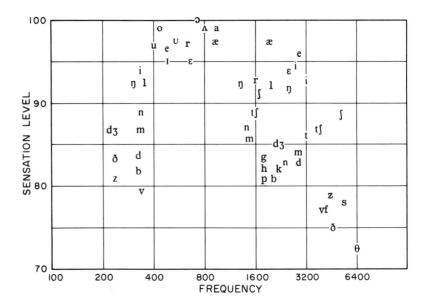

FIGURE 3. *Intensity and frequency characteristics of some of the fundamental sounds of speech. (R. Irwin transposition chart from H. Fletcher, Speech and Hearing in Communication, Bell Telephone Laboratories, Inc., copyright 1953, D. Van Nostrand Co., Inc., p. 87.)*

Test W-22. The scores resulting from administration of these lists are scores that show percentage of correct discrimination. The point must be reemphasized, however, that these tests yield measures relating to hearing function, not handicap. There has been an effort to work out a set of measures called the Social Adequacy Index,[2] based on both the discrimination scores obtained in testing with the PB's and speech reception scores obtained in testing for the speech reception threshold. This index has probably been the most effective set of measures yet devised to help quantify the communication handicap associated with hearing loss. When hearing loss interferes with communication, it may well influence success or failure of children in school.

SCHOOL ADJUSTMENT

It is difficult to make generalizations about school problems arising as a result of hearing loss without becoming more definitive about categories of loss. Those with hearing loss within schools present a heterogeneous group, ranging from very slight to profound losses. One does not suspect that the loss of a slight amount of hearing will have the same effect on school achievement as the loss of a greater magnitude. Therefore,

[2] H. Davis, "The Articulation Area and the Social Adequacy Index for Hearing," *Laryngoscope*, (1948), 58:761–78.

the approach to the education of the child with a hearing loss will, in large measure, depend on the severity of the loss. That hearing deficit can affect performance on tests employed to determine mental ability comes as no surprise, particularly if the tests employed are highly dependent on usage of oral language. The most effective tests for children with hearing loss are those that measure intelligence through performance that is not dependent on oral language.

There is no question that the greatest problems in making the school experience a successful one for the child with hearing loss are those associated with communication. All possible sensory avenues that can aid the child's learning should be used in the teaching-learning process. The individualized approach necessary in the education of the child with hearing loss might be undertaken within the public school classroom, a day school program, or a residential school. The location is of minor consequence as long as the program is geared to meet the varying needs of the heterogeneous group of children who sustain hearing loss.

In her discussion of the general educational aspects of hearing loss, Streng[3] establishes classifications that could well serve as points of departure in the formulation of a special school program for children with hearing losses. The classifications are as follows:

Class 1. They are the children with mild losses (20–30 db in the better ear in the speech range). They learn speech by ear and are on the borderline between the normally hearing and those with significant defective hearing.

Class 2. They are the children with marginal losses (30–40 db). They have difficulty understanding speech by ear at a distance of more than a few feet and in following group conversation.

Class 3. They are the children with moderate losses (40–60 db). They have enough hearing to learn language and speech through the ear when sound is amplified for them and when the auditory sense is aided by the visual.

The children in these first three categories may be considered as being hard of hearing.

Class 4. They are the children with severe losses (60–75 db). They have trainable residual hearing but their language and speech will not develop spontaneously, so they must learn to communicate through the use of specialized techniques. They are on the borderline between the hard of hearing and the deaf, and may be considered the "educationally deaf" or partially deaf.

Class 5. They are the children with profound losses (greater than 75 db). They cannot learn to understand language by ear alone, even with the amplification of sound.

---

[3] A. Streng, *et. al., Hearing Therapy for Children* 2nd rev. ed. (New York: Grune and Stratton, Inc., 1958), pp. 164–65. Reprinted by permission of the author and publisher.

Living organisms tend to alter their response patterns as conditions about them change. Also, modification of the organism by external or internal forces tends to result in different response patterns if the modification threatens the existence of the organism. This shift in response patterns is commonly referred to as adjustment. Two areas of adjustment are (1) the adjustment of the organism to itself and (2) the adjustment of the organism to the world in which it exists. These two areas of adjustment are not unrelated but will be treated separately.

The self-adjustment of any individual with hearing loss will be affected by a number of factors. They are (1) amount of loss, (2) age at onset of loss, (3) suddenness of the loss, (4) reaction of others to the loss, (5) personality structure prior to the onset of the loss, (6) motivation to overcome the effects of the loss, and (7) help from others in overcoming the effects of the loss.

AMOUNT OF LOSS

One would expect that the self-adjustment of an individual who sustains a slight-to-moderate loss of hearing would be substantially different from one who has lost all his hearing. One with only a slight or moderate loss still relates auditorally to his environment and thereby monitors his behavior accordingly; whereas one who has no residual hearing must rely solely on reports brought to him through other sensory channels to monitor his behavior. Since he cannot see around corners or feel unless he makes actual physical contact, there are environmental stimuli to which he cannot respond meaningfully. Thus his behavior is different, and subsequent self-evaluation of that behavior changes.

AGE AT ONSET OF LOSS

If one suffers a loss of hearing very early in life, his problems are different from one who loses his hearing at a later age. If, for example, language has not yet been learned, there is the tremendous task of coping with this area of learning that is so closely tied to other areas of development. The child born without hearing or one who loses it in the early years is faced with a basic problem of adjustment at the outset; however, the older child or adult who loses his hearing is faced with learning new and different patterns of adjustment. In a sense he must unlearn some of the old responses and then learn new ones. The transitional period can have disquieting effects, not only because habit patterns become firmly fixed, but also because the human organism tends to resist change.

SUDDENNESS OF THE LOSS

As sensory function is gradually reduced, the human organism gradually adapts to the reduction and thereby assists in the total adjustment-process. However, when the sensory receptor is abruptly deprived of stimulation, there is no time for adequate adaptation and hence a state of disequilibrium exists. Often the person who has lost his hearing over a period of years will present himself for audiological evaluation at the urging of a wife or husband. The loss frequently concerns him less than those about him. What has happened is that he has gradually learned to live without the assistance of an intact auditory mechanism. Upon providing amplification to this type of hearing loss case, remarks such as "Golly, I really didn't remember there were such noises all around" or "Hmm, I had forgotten that one can hear himself breathe" are forthcoming.

When hearing loss occurs suddenly in adults, the effects can be quite traumatic in terms of adjustment. The person has been suddenly burdened not only with problems directly associated with communication but also with problems of adjustment to the environment outside the realm of human communication. No longer are the taxi horn, the dog's bark, the twelve o'clock whistle, and so forth, a part of the daily experience. Ramsdell[4] suggests that there is associated with deafness a more basic and severe impairment than that encountered in communication. This impairment is one of depression. Only insight into, and an understanding of, the feelings of depression will provide those suffering from sudden hearing loss with a brighter outlook.

REACTION OF OTHERS TO THE LOSS

The evaluation of self, in large measure, is affected by an individual's perceptions of the evaluations of himself by others. Since this is true, it is fairly easy to see that overconcern on the part of others could contribute to a growing feeling of inadequacy and insecurity. Likewise, total lack of concern by others could affect adversely one's self-adjustment pattern and thereby materially affect one's self-concept. One of the real problems which the clinician considers is that of the reactions and appraisals of those who are close to the person suffering hearing loss. For when the individual with hearing loss is reacted to as being "different," it is likely

---

[4] H. Davis and S. R. Silverman, *Hearing and Deafness,* rev. ed. (New York: Holt, Rinehart and Winston, Inc., 1960), p. 459.

that he will eventually evaluate himself as being different and make responses that are appropriate to this evaluation.

PERSONALITY STRUCTURE PRIOR TO ONSET OF LOSS

Although the emotionally stable person who sustains a sudden shock of deafness may work hard to cope with its effects, the telling effects of the blow on the person's self-adjustment are frequently obvious. However, the person who has been somewhat emotionally unstable before the loss often presents problems of self-adjustment, because hearing loss seems to add to feelings of fear and lack of self-confidence.

MOTIVATION TO OVERCOME EFFECTS OF THE LOSS

As is true in attempting to solve any kind of problem, the desire to combat the effects of hearing loss can contribute greatly to adjustment to the loss. Many times the writer has observed in clinical work with persons having hearing loss, that those who are highly motivated to succeed in overcoming the problems of hearing loss are able to do so. As they succeed they live more happily with themselves and others. Those with little or no motivation to overcome the effects of hearing loss frequently waste their time and the time of the clinician. It is a challenge to the clinician to stimulate the motivation and the desire of the hard of hearing to improve.

HELP FROM OTHERS IN OVERCOMING THE EFFECTS OF THE LOSS

The self-adjustment of the hard of hearing can be greatly enhanced by intelligent cooperation of those within the immediate environment. Their attempt to make their faces visible to the hard-of-hearing listener is only one way—but a very important one—to help. In many such ways they can contribute to the feelings of *success* and *belonging* on the part of the hard of hearing. The effects of others in the self-adjustment of the hard of hearing must never be underestimated, and the effective clinician will try to determine the attitudes of wives, husbands, children, and other close associates toward his client.

SOCIAL ADJUSTMENT

One of the outstanding problems associated with hearing loss is that of social adjustment. The problems are frequently far less for the child born with a hearing impairment that is identified early than for the child who sustains a hearing loss that is not recognized until his performance in school leads someone to suspect that "perhaps he doesn't hear well." Too frequently the child fitting this latter description is considered slow if not mentally retarded.

Hearing loss in childhood, depending upon the severity, can serve to cause withdrawal in work and play situations at school and at home. It is the normal, easy give-and-take of language communication among humans that helps to relate them to the ongoing stream of events. Because he is unaware of the attitudes of those about him toward the social milieu in which he exists, the hard-of-hearing client tends to respond in a more independent and perhaps less socially acceptable manner. This nonconforming type of behavior, which he logically exhibits, serves to mark him as being different. When viewed as being different, the responses toward him are altered, and thus he becomes "funny," "odd," "stupid," and so on.

In the case of adults who lose the sense of hearing, too frequently there is a withdrawal from situations of which they had formerly been an integral part. Generally the feeling is that because of the reduction of auditory sensitivity they simply cannot "keep up" with the demands made upon them. As the hard-of-hearing person begins to believe this, and responds accordingly, so do those about him. They too respond as if their friend had "slipped." The writer will never forget the woman who came to him for audiological evaluation at the behest of her husband. There were signs of withdrawal, as she told how her deafness was "taking the joy out of life" and causing her to "give up many of the social activities" that she had previously enjoyed. It so happened that the writer also knew several of her friends, one of whom had commented sadly on her friend's deafness, and how people were accepting the fact of her handicap and didn't "count on her" for many of the activities in which she had previously participated. The results of the test were very surprising and so the woman was retested. The results showed that she sustained only a very slight loss for the high frequencies in both ears. When told of the very minor loss of hearing she sustained, the woman was overjoyed. The story shows that the woman's attitude toward her "deafness" caused a change in her behavior, which was radiated to those about her. Those about her likewise then changed their behavior toward her. One's degree of self-adjustment can affect the attitudes of others toward him and in turn can cause him to behave differently toward others as he perceives their attitudes and evaluations. The great problem for the clinician is to determine the extent to which the problem of social adjustment contributes to the handicap of a hearing loss.

VOCATIONAL ADJUSTMENT

The greatest problems of vocational adjustment for the person with hearing loss stem from those situations where vocational success depends on communication. Much is being done for the deaf person in need of vocational help. Schools for the deaf have for years included vocational programs for boys and girls. More recently, federal money has become available for studying the vocational needs and capabilities of the deaf. To cite an example, a research program of interest and merit carried on by the Michigan Association for Better Hearing, and sponsored by the Vocational Rehabilitation of the Department of Health, Education, and Welfare, has as its objective the determination of factors contributing to the failure of deaf men to adjust in vocational situations.

Frequently it is the hard-of-hearing person, with moderate-to-severe loss, who finds it very difficult to make good vocational adjustment. He is not a deaf man and no one may even suspect that he is having difficulty hearing. Wishing to hide his problem, he may use various devices to keep it a secret. The writer is reminded of the man who kept a radio blaring in his office, so that anyone who came in virtually had to shout in order to be understood. The device worked, but it set him apart as being the "odd duck with the blaring radio."

The skillful clinician will determine whether or not his hard-of-hearing client is having problems at work because of his loss of hearing. If so, proper steps should be taken to understand more fully the dynamics of the situation. If vocational counseling is necessary, proper liaison should be set up with a vocational counselor.

In view of the many problems that can be associated with hearing loss, it should behoove the clinician to determine with more precision the relative contribution of the problems to the total picture, thereby constructing a frame of reference against which to carry out a meaningful program of habilitation or rehabilitation. The handicap that attends hearing loss will, in the main, have to be determined on an individual basis. For the handicap varies with the total adjustment that is made.

SUMMARY

In this chapter emphasis has been placed on the different problems that attend loss of hearing. The difference between hearing loss and hearing handicap was stressed. It was pointed out that hearing loss and hearing handicap do not have a one-to-one relationship. The area of handicap in communication probably presents the greatest concern to the clinician. Scholastic progress depends greatly on the severity of the loss, and successful communication is a large factor affecting progress.

Self-adjustment was discussed with special reference to the amount of loss, age at onset of loss, suddenness of the loss, reaction of others, personality of the hard-of-hearing individual, motivation, and help from others in overcoming the effects of hearing loss. The dynamics of social and vocational adjustment were discussed.

4

TO UNDERSTAND THE AUDITORY TRAINING PROC-
ess more completely, it is important that the student learn about the perception of sounds. To
place the perception of sounds in proper perspec-
tive, some facts relating to (1) basic concepts of
human perception, (2) auditory perception of
nonspeech stimuli, and (3) perception of speech
will be discussed briefly. The intent is to provide
sufficient background so that the student may ap-
preciate more fully the problems he will encounter
in attempting to administer training to one with
auditory deficit.

BASIC CONCEPTS OF HUMAN PERCEPTION

Perception is not easily defined although some
attempts have been made to do so. William James[1]
in 1892 defined perception as "consciousness of

[1] W. James, *Principles of Psychology* (New York: Holt, Rinehart
and Winston, Inc., 1892), p. 312.

AUDITORY
PERCEPTION

particular material things present to sense." Thirty-two years later, Sea-shore[2] suggested that "sensation and perception together constitute sensory experience." Boring and colleagues[3] have suggested that perception is the first event in the chain that leads from stimulation to response of the organism, that it is the experience of objects that are here, now, and further that it is a response to some change or difference in the environment.

A somewhat more general definition offered by Stagner and Karwoski[4] characterizes perception as being the process through which a knowledge of external objects and events is accomplished through the senses. Goldiamond,[5] in a discussion of the definitions of perception, points out the importance of procedural adequacy in perception experiments and suggests that the extent of relationship of experimental findings to perception depends on the adequacy of the procedures utilized. Many more definitions could be reproduced here but would not necessarily prove valuable in this discussion.

Generally, the older definitions were relatively fragmentary and vague and did not lead to a much greater understanding of the perceptual process. Bartley[6] in his thorough treatment of the topic, points out that "perception is the overall activity of the organism that immediately follows or accompanies energistic impingements upon the sense organs." It is the work of the sensory mechanism to mediate between the internal activities of the organism and those events external to it. In the mediation process the stimulus is detected, transformed into nerve impulses, and then related to patterns previously organized by the organism. It should be emphasized that a study of this process provides information concerning the experience of the organism as it is stimulated by the outside world but yields no data about the stimuli provided from the outside. Two concepts, important to understanding perception, are those of immediacy and discrimination.[7] If the organism is said to perceive, it does so immediately as stimuli impinge upon it. As it perceives, it selectively reacts to stimuli—or discriminates. In other words there is a time limit within which the system responds to and selects among

---

[2] C. Seashore, *Introduction to Psychology* (New York: The Macmillan Company, 1924), p. 9.

[3] E. G. Boring, H. Langfeld and H. P. Weld, *Foundations of Psychology* (New York: John Wiley & Sons, Inc., 1948), pp. 215–17.

[4] R. Stagner and T. Karwoski, *Psychology* (New York: McGraw-Hill Book Company, 1952), p. 207.

[5] I. Goldiamond, "Perception," Chapter 9 in *Experimental Foundations of Clinical Psychology*, A. J. Bachrach, ed. (New York: Basic Books, Inc., 1962), pp. 305–6.

[6] S. H. Bartley, *Principles of Perception* (New York: Harper and Row, Publishers, Inc., 1957), p. 22.

[7] Bartley, *ibid.*, p. 22.

stimuli as it perceives. Reflexive responses that are characterized by discrimination involve participation of the cerebral cortex and are to be viewed as a form of perceptual behavior.

Hudgins[8] viewed perception as a synthesis of information that is fed to the organism from several sensory avenues simultaneously. He emphasized the fact that the sensory modalities are not compartmentalized but that one modality may dominate the process. Thus, as the organism is stimulated, the appropriate sensory receptor picks up the energy of the stimulus and transmits it along the sensory pathway in neural impulses to the cortex, at which level a patterning occurs. The patterns are related to previous ones and hence are determined to be similar or dissimilar. Following discrimination of similarity or dissimilarity and integration of the decisions made, perception occurs. The response given by the subject following this process is called his *judgment*.

ATTITUDES TOWARD PERCEPTION

In his discussion of perceptual organization, Osgood[9] suggests that there are three attitudes toward perceptual phenomena: (1) the physiological, (2) the gestalt, and (3) the behavioristic. It would appear that the first point of view attempts to explain perception on the basis of observable neurophysiological mechanisms. This approach demands full explanation of the handling of the stimulus at the peripheral level. With this accomplished, however, the question still remains concerning function at a central level, for it is at the cortical level that perceiving takes place. The painstaking scientific description of peripheral function does provide, however, a real basis for understanding the function of the higher centers in handling the stimulus. Even though considerable neurophysiological experimentation has taken place in the area of audition, continued effort in this direction should yield a more scientific basis than we presently have, upon which to prescribe auditory training procedures.

The proponent of the gestalt view employs a molar approach in explaining physiological processes underlying perception. A symmetrical neural patterning upon stimulation is thought to occur because of the many interconnections among nerve cells. By postulating this sort of interdependence among fibers, it is quite logical for gestalt followers to assume that effort to explain the functioning neural processes in a molecular manner is not too worthwhile. Rather, they postulate field forces as an explanation of the neurophysiological processes that operate in percep-

---

[8] C. V. Hudgins, "Auditory Training: Its Possibilities and Limitations," *The Volta Bureau,* Reprint No. 652, p. 2.

[9] C. E. Osgood, *Method and Theory in Experimental Psychology* (New York: Oxford University Press, 1953), p. 195.

tion. The failure to specify precisely where the forces operate within the brain tends to make this approach a rather vague one in any attempt to understand perception fully.

The behavioristic approach to perception is primarily that of describing responses. It is difficult, if not impossible, to incorporate into the major constructs of *S–R* (*stimulus* and *response*) any detailed explanation of perception. For within this framework, perceptual events are mediation processes. The general approach is gross and promises little as far as detailed explanation of perception. Even though a rigorous neurophysiological approach would appear to be the most plausible way of trying to understand the perceptual process, there is little question that observations carefully made by those of differing orientations should also help contribute to a solution of this very complex problem.

Knowledge derived from perception experiments in vision, taste, smell, and the somesthetic senses is extensive and important for understanding the perceptual process. The methodology and also the interrelationships of the central mechanisms responsible for perceptions are of particular interest. It is not the purpose of this chapter to explore these but to discuss the general topic of auditory perception and then more specifically the perception of the acoustic component of speech.

AUDITORY PERCEPTION OF NONSPEECH STIMULI

A human characteristic is to take for granted the proper functioning of the senses, until for some reason we are made aware of malfunction in ourselves or someone around us. The slam of a door, the hum of a motor, the toot of a horn, the rush of water, and thousands of other sounds pervade our lives daily. We attend to the multitude of sounds about us with varying degrees of responsiveness. Those that signal danger command our immediate attention. Those that help to keep us time oriented, such as the strike of a clock or ringing of a bell, may be answered with somewhat less urgency. Of course there are those sounds which we hardly notice; but when they cease, we become conscious of the fact that they are no longer present.

A sound must be received to be perceived. Perception of sound, any sound, depends on whether or not it is within the limits of the human system. Roughly, the frequency limits for normals are from 16 cps to 16,000–20,000 cps. Higher or lower frequencies are not perceived as sounds. In terms of intensity, the lower limits vary according to frequency —that is, to be heard certain frequencies require more energy than others. (Figure 4 .presents the auditory area.) The upper limits for intensity, as shown in Figure 4, vary from 120 db to 140 db. At 140 db, sounds

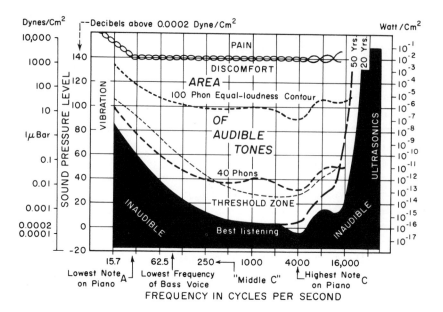

FIGURE 4. The auditory area. (From H. Davis and S. R. Silverman, Hearing and Deafness, rev. ed. (New York: Holt, Rinehart and Winston, Inc., 1960), p. 46.

induce pain. On the assumption that the student has covered the structure and function of the hearing mechanism, hearing problems, and hearing measurement before studying rehabilitation, discussion of these aspects is unnecessary here. The process of the perception of sound can be conceptualized in terms of sound discrimination or differentiation and sound identification. The differentiation aspect is that which is commonly referred to as discrimination.

SOUND DISCRIMINATION

Discrimination of sounds refers to the sorting and sifting out of sounds from each other. This involves comparison of the heard sound with other sounds that are competing. It also involves selection from among those sounds that have been a part of the experiential background of the auditor. Regarding determination of the neural basis of audition, Neff and Diamond[10] state that one of the oldest methods of studying the brain and behavior is that of observing behavior of animals before and after selective ablation of neural areas. In other words, it is a way

[10] W. D. Neff and I. T. Diamond, "The Neural Basis of Auditory Discrimination," in H. F. Harlow and C. Woolsey, eds., Biological and Biochemical Bases of Behavior (Madison, Wisc.: The University of Wisconsin Press, 1958), pp. 101–26.

of determining how pitch, loudness, duration, and other kinds of discriminations are changed when a specified portion of the central nervous system is destroyed.

Ablation studies concerned with sound localization, frequency discrimination, and pattern discrimination help to explain the general topic of auditory discrimination. Regarding sound localization in space, Neff and Diamond[11] experimented with cats and found that when they were deprived of the auditory cortex, they could not appropriately use the patterns of nerve impulses set up in lower brain centers when the two ears are stimulated by a single-sound source. Furthermore, the animals cannot maintain attention to acoustic signals, and over a period of time their behavior cannot be guided by sounds. Discrimination of frequency, however, has been shown to be little affected by bilateral ablation. Their experimentation with the role of the auditory cortex and pattern discrimination tends to indicate that only a small amount of cortex is necessary for the cat to relearn pattern discrimination.

When auditory discriminations can be made after portions of or all the auditory cortex has been destroyed, the only reasonable conclusion is that new neural units are excited as the sounds are presented. Some people who have worked with the brain injured have casually referred to this kind of activity as the rerouting of impulses. Based on neurophysiological studies of ablation of the auditory cortex, it has been suggested that it is possible to make certain predictions concerning ablation and discrimination. Although he has not investigated experimentally, Neff[12] suggests that bilateral ablation of the auditory cortex will cause severe loss in discrimination for change in the repetition rate of an acoustic signal. This would affect pitch perception. The neurophysiological approach holds much promise for better understanding of and keener insights into the behavior and problems of the auditorially handicapped. Further experimentation is needed, however, before the many psychophysical data already available can be explained on a neurophysiological level.

Turning now to the psychophysical approach, we find that much information concerning sound discrimination is available. First of all, it should be noted that the human auditory system is capable of discriminating among many sounds of varying frequencies and intensities. Figure 5[13] presents a picture of the number of distinguishable tones within

[11] *Ibid.,* p. 102.

[12] W. D. Neff, "Role of the Auditory Cortex in Sound Discrimination," Chapter 15 in G. L. Rasmussen and W. F. Windle, eds., *Neural Mechanisms of the Auditory and Vestibular Systems* (Springfield, Ill.: Charles C. Thomas, Publisher, 1960), pp. 215–16.

[13] S. S. Stevens and H. Davis, *Hearing: Its Psychology and Physiology* (New York: John Wiley & Sons, Inc., 1954), pp. 152–54.

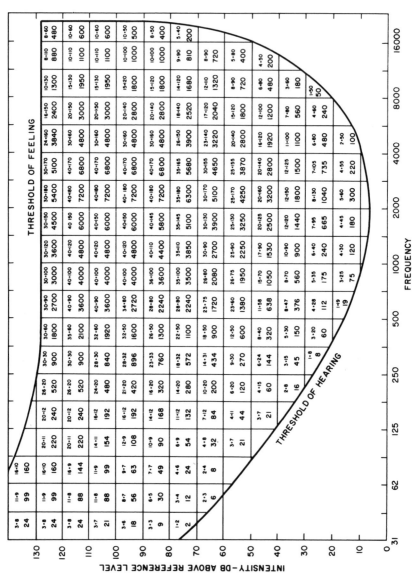

FIGURE 5. Distinguishable tones within the human range of audition. The first number gives the height of the cell in difference-limens for intensity and the second number gives the difference-limens for frequency. The number written directly below is the product of the two numbers. (From S.S. Stevens, H. Davis, Hearing: Its Psychology and Physiology. New York: John Wiley and Sons, Inc., 1938, p. 153.)

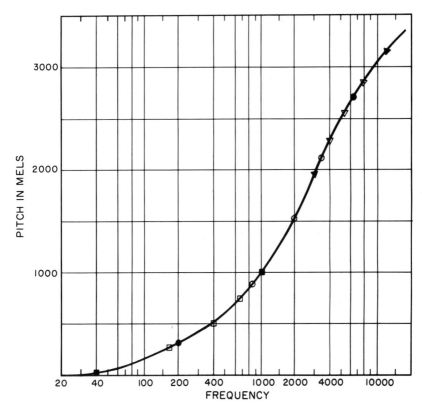

FIGURE 6. *Relationship of pitch in mels to frequency. The circles, squares, and triangles represent data in the experiment on equal sense-distances. Filled figures mark ends of three frequency-ranges, hollow figures show points arrived at when observers divided the ranges into four equal intervals of pitch. (S. S. Stevens, J. Volkmann, "The Relation of Pitch to Frequency : A Revised Scale," The American Journal of Psychology (1940), III : 336.)*

the range of human audition. There are approximately 340,000 distinguishable tones the human ear can hear (1500 "just noticeable differences" for pitch and 325 "just noticeable differences" for loudness).

In order to determine the responses of human subjects to sounds, it is necessary to rely on proven psychophysical methods. Since the responses of subjects vary from moment to moment, it is imperative that responses be recorded over a period of time and then subjected to statistical analyses. Using this approach, one is able to state with reasonable confidence the probability of obtaining certain responses when the conditions under which the stimulus is presented are held constant. The most important attributes of tones investigated have been pitch (for pure and complex sounds), loudness, duration, volume, density, brightness, two-ear versus one-ear listening, and masking.

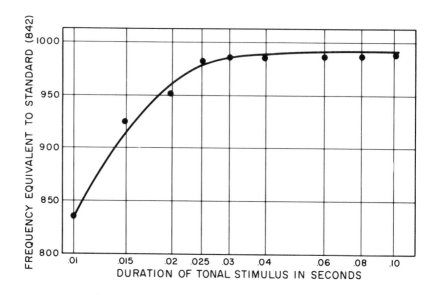

FIGURE 7. *Tonal duration and pitch. Each point represents the average of 60 observa-tions by a single observer. (From S.S. Stevens, H. Davis, Hearing : Its Psychology and Physiology, New York : John Wiley and Sons, Inc., 1938, p. 101.)*

Pitch of Pure Tones. Pitch varies most with reference to frequency of the tone. In the main, high frequencies are heard as high pitches and low frequencies as low pitches. In 1937 two investigators[14] constructed a scale for the measurement of perceived pitches of sounds. The unit of measure-ment for pitch was called the *mel.* One thousand mels is the pitch heard when a 1000-cps tone is heard at 40 decibels (re: 0.0002 dyne/cm²). Figure 6 shows the graph that was plotted which relates pitch in mels to frequency. It will be observed that from about 1000 cps upward the relationship between frequency and observed pitch is almost a linear one.

Pitch of Complex Tones. It was observed by Fletcher[15] that a complex tone, composed of frequencies which differed by a constant amount, would result in a pitch which was judged to be the same as the amount by which they differed, rather than the amount represented by a mean of the components. For example, a complex tone of 500, 600, and 700 cps would have a pitch perceived to be 100 cps. Whereas a tone of 200,

[14] S. S. Stevens, J. Volkman, "The Relation of Pitch to Frequency: A Revised Scale," *The American Journal of Psychology* (1940), III: 336.

[15] H. Fletcher, "Loudness, Pitch and Timbre of Musical Tones and Their Relation to the Intensity, the Frequency and the Over-Tone Structure," *Journal of the Acoustical Society of America,* 6: 59–69.

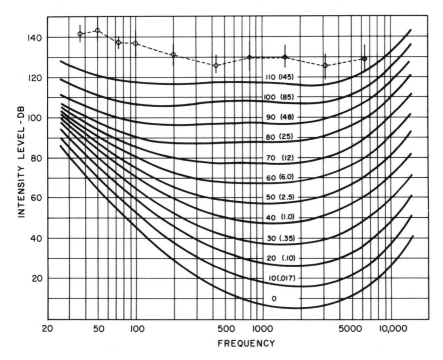

FIGURE 8. *Equal-loudness contours as a function of intensity (db above reference-pressure). The Wegel data for feeling threshold represented at top by dotted curve. The first of the two numbers on the contour lines shows loudness-level and the number in parentheses shows loudness in sones. (From S.S. Stevens and H. Davis, Hearing: Its Psychology and Physiology, New York: John Wiley and Sons, Inc., 1938, p. 124.)*

400, and 600 cps would be perceived as a tone with a pitch of 200 cps.

Pitch and Length of Tone. The length of time that a tone is presented has a direct effect on its perceived pitch. Stevens and Davis[16] point up graphically (Figure 7) the relationship between tonal duration and perceived pitch. Between 250 cps and 8000 cps, as a tone is shortened the pitch falls.

Loudness. The loudness of a tone is dependent not only on the amount of energy with which it is presented but also on its frequency. The sone is the unit of loudness, and the relationships that exist among sounds of the various frequencies are shown in Figure 8. This graphic display is called "equal loudness contours." The zero contour (lowest line in the figure) presents a curve for minimum audible sound pressure. This line shows that a sound of 1000 cps at threshold calls for substantially less energy or intensity than does a sound of 100 cps. Note that the relation-

16 Stevens and Davis, *Hearing: Its Psychology and Physiology*, p. 101.

ship changes, however, for the 1000-cps tone as it is presented at levels above threshold. (The first number on the lines shows decibels above threshold and the second the loudness in sones.) Thus we can say that there is a differential perception of loudness of a tone as a function of frequency as well as intensity.

Loudness and Length of Tone. Just as in the judgment of pitch, the length of the tone makes a difference in the judgment of loudness. Loudness increases as duration increases up to a point and then levels off. Licklider[17] has contributed information on this point.

Volume of Sound. Volume is a term that is used frequently by those who really mean *intensity*. The volume controls on radios and television sets add to the confusion. The term volume refers to the "bigness" or "smallness" of a sound. A low note on a piano seems to occupy more space or to be "bigger" than a high note. In 1934 Stevens[18] scaled the attribute of volume and constructed equal-volume contours. It must be remembered that volume increases with increase in loudness and decreases with increase in pitch. The perceived volume or "bigness" of a sound can be kept constant by manipulation of pitch and intensity.

Brightness and Density of Sound. It would appear that the terms brightness and density are two different words referring to the same tonal attribute. Some early attempts indicated that they are quite separate and distinct attributes, but later work does not reinforce this position.[19, 20]

Two-ear versus One-ear Listening. There are some distinguishable differences in the perception of sound with the use of only one or both ears.

In terms of binaural versus monaural effects on human threshold, there is evidence that two-ear listening results in a threshold that is 6 db lower than that achieved in one-ear listening. Summation of nervous excitations apparently occurs at threshold or perhaps below threshold, thus resulting in a lower value when two ears are utilized than when only one is employed. Not only is hearing threshold lower with two-ear participation, but auditory discrimination is finer for both frequency and intensity.

The study of the ability to locate the source of sounds presents some

---

[17] J.C.R. Licklider, "Basic Correlates of the Auditory Stimulus," Chapter 25 in S. S. Stevens, ed., *Handbook of Experimental Psychology* (New York: John Wiley & Sons, Inc., 1953), p. 985.

[18] S. S. Stevens, "The Volume and Intensity of Tones," *American Journal of Psychology* (1934), 6:397–408.

[19] S. S. Stevens, "The Attributes of Tones," *Proceedings of the National Academy of Science* (1934), 20:457–59.

[20] S. S. Stevens, "Tonal Density," *Journal of Experimental Psychology* (1934), 17:585–92.

rather interesting results. It has been found that (1) persons can locate tones more accurately than noises; (2) sources located to the right and left can be distinguished with great accuracy; (3) there is confusion about the location of sounds lying in the median plane; and (4) persons are least accurate in detecting small changes in the azimuth of sounds that are produced directly from the sides. In general, errors in localization are usually few and constant at low frequencies but increase as the tone is raised to near 3000 cps. After 4000 cps the localization improves and is as accurate at 10,000 cps as at 1000 cps.[21]

Phase provides an effective cue to the localization of tones. Phase differences are present in the pressure waves in the right- and left-ear canals, as the sound source is located either to the right or left of the listener's head. For if the source is located to the left of a listener, the path of the sound is longer to the right ear than to the left and vice versa. Thus temporal cues contribute to the success in sound localization. The relative intensity gives excellent cues for localizing high but not low tones. When sounds of a complex nature are presented for localization, they are easily localized because phase differences are provided by the low frequencies and intensity differences by the high tones. In fact, one is almost as successful in localizing complex tones when using one ear as when using two ears.[22]

SOUND IDENTIFICATION

One can make many judgments about sound, as pointed out by the preceding paragraphs. How loud or how soft, how high or how low, how long or how short, how bright or how dull, or the direction from which sound originates represent some of the discriminatory judgments one can make. Indeed it is possible to make these judgments and yet be unable to specify the sound's origin. To specify the origin is a matter of identification.

The process of identification of sound is one in which the sorting and sifting involved in discrimination occurs. But in addition the listener is called on to relate the sound he hears to past experiences or present surroundings. This places a different kind of demand on the listener. Recently the writer had an experience that illustrates the point. He had retired for the night and all lights were out. Suddenly there was a cracking noise that seemed to come from either the living room or dining room. The sounds were of short duration and occurred irregularly with

---

[21] Stevens and Davis, *Hearing: Its Psychology and Physiology,* p. 178.
[22] *Ibid.,* p. 180.

no more than five seconds between them. They were moderately loud and sharp or bright. No pitch level was associated with them. Yet after making all these discriminations, it was impossible to determine the origin of the sound. It really sounded like someone breaking a wooden ruler over his knee or perhaps loading a shotgun. And then light was literally shed upon the mystery, as the hall and living room became bright with light from the fireplace. The cracking noise was caused by a piece of firewood that had been smoldering for several hours and suddenly burst into flame. The problem of sound identification can be quite difficult for the person with normal hearing but can present even more problems for the hearing-handicapped person, particularly if sound distortion is a complicating factor.

PERCEPTION OF SPEECH

From the standpoint of acoustics, one can view the sounds that comprise the words used in human communication in the same way as any other complex acoustic event. In the analysis of speech, the factors of intensity, frequency, and time and their interrelationships are considered just as they are in the analysis of sound produced by a siren or bell. However, as words tumble upon our ears, one after another, we frequently need to perceive only a part of what has been said to understand. There is a peculiar and distinct relationship among the acoustic events that we call words that does not exist for the many other sounds to which the listener is subjected.

As one examines speech in a somewhat molecular fashion, it soon becomes evident that there are many individual differences among talkers. In other words, they show considerable variability in their performances, particularly as they speak in backgrounds of interfering noise. In spite of this, however, the speech signal can be considered a very durable signal as shown by quantitative investigation.

Rigorous assessment of speech was carried out early by the Bell Telephone Laboratories. They were concerned principally with performance of equipment and utilized speakers and listeners to accomplish their end. In their measurement of speech power, they determined that there were quite striking differences among the various sounds of speech. Table I shows the relationships among the sounds in microwatts.[23] It was further noted that the difference between the faintest whisper and loudest shout was 60 db. The average conversational speech is approximately 10–20

[23] C. F. Sacia and C. F. Beck, "The Power of Fundamental Speech Sounds," *Bell System Technical Journal* (1926), 5:393–403.

TABLE I. *Relationship Among Sounds in Microwatts.*

Phonetic Sound	Key Word	Phonetic Power		Peak Power		Calculations from Threshold and Articulation Measurements
		Average	*Maximum*	*Average*	*Maximum*	
ū	tool	23	60	235	700	38
u	took	26	100	470	890	50
ō	tone	25	80	435	1300	74
o′	talk	45	120	615	1500	87
o	ton	24	110	450	1700	83
a	top	41	120	700	1600	68
á	tap	25	90	650	1800	57
e	ten	22	90	500	1700	34
ā	tape	23	60	525	1700	35
i	tip	20	50	350	1300	22
ē	team	20	80	310	1500	16
m	me	1.8	17	110	200	2.9
n	no	2.1	18	47	70	4.1
ng	ring	.3	3.6	97	170	12
l	let	.3	9.6	130	230	18
r	err	16	30	200	600	33
v	vat	.03	2.4	25	30	1.0
f	for	.08	3.6	3	4	1.0
z	zip	.7	7.2	30	40	1.2
s	sit	.9	8.7	30	55	.9
th	thin			1	1	.3
th	that			9	10	2.3
zh	azure			40	55	
sh	shot	1.8	6.0	110	130	11
b	bat			7	7	1.1
p	pat			6	7	1.0
d	dot	.08	2.9	4	7	1.7
t	tap	.1	6.0	16	19	2.7
j	jot	.5	3.6	24	36	4.1
ch	chat	1.4	19	52	60	6.1
g	get			8	9	3.3
k	kit	.3	4.8	6	9	3.0

microwatts. Conversational speech can be viewed also as producing energy equal to 125 ergs per second. Ten million ergs per second are equal to one watt. Imagine the speech energy necessary to light a 40-watt bulb which required 400 million ergs per second. It has been shown that men have on the average about twice the energy in their speech as women.[24]

Davis[25] has shown that 33 db is necessary for understanding 50 per cent

[24] H. Fletcher, *Speech and Hearing in Communication* (Princeton, N.J.: D. Van Nostrand Co., Inc., 1953), p. 76.
[25] H. Davis, *Hearing and Deafness* (New York: Murray Hill, 1947), p. 150.

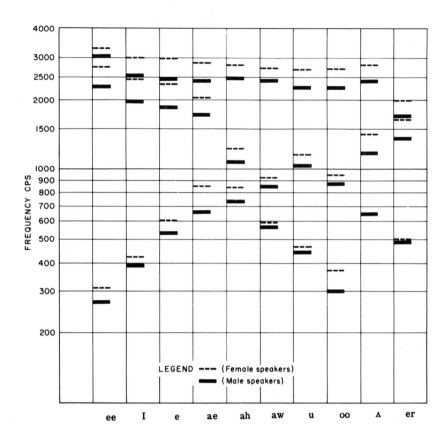

FIGURE 9. *Mean values for formants of 10 English vowels. (From P. B. Denes and E. N. Pinson,* The Speech Chain, *Courtesy of Bell Telephone Laboratories, Inc., 1963, p. 118.)*

of the monosyllables he presented through earphones and that the spondees need but 22 db for 50 per cent recognition. Connected speech can be understood when the level is 24 db. The frequency component of speech is fascinating and important to the audiologist engaged in auditory training. The vowels of speech are distributed as shown in Figure 9.[26] Note the different points at which energy is concentrated for each of the vowels. Figure 10[27] presents a picture of the longtime average spectrum of speech. If one were to lay a straight edge from the midpoint between 500 cps and 1000 cps to the top of the figure, he would find more energy in the low frequencies than in the high frequencies as a function of time.

[26] P. B. Denes and E. N. Pinson, *The Speech Chain* (Bell Telephone Laboratories, Inc., 1963), p. 118.
[27] *Ibid.*, p. 116.

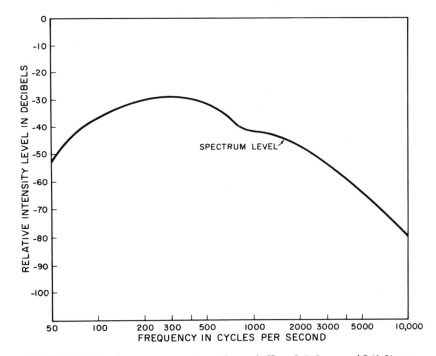

FIGURE 10. *Longtime average spectrum of speech. (From P. B. Denes and E. N. Pinson, The Speech Chain, Courtesy of Bell Telephone Laboratories, Inc., p. 116.)*

The question arises concerning the part the low, middle, and high frequencies play in understanding speech. Figure 11[28] illustrates the fact that as much intelligibility results from frequencies below 1900 cps as above this point. As far as the masking of speech by interfering sounds is concerned, low-frequency tones are much more interfering than are higher tones. Generally, masking is most effective at or above the frequency of the masking tone.[29]

Reverberation, when severe, interferes seriously with the correct perception of speech. When the architecture of a room causes reverberation, well-articulated speech becomes muffled, blurred speech. Studies abound that are directed toward measuring the perception of speech of normal-hearing subjects in conditions of quiet and noise. There have been fewer studies made of the perception of speech by the hearing handicapped. There are several measures that should be made of the hearing-handi-

---

[28] J.C.R. Licklider and George A. Miller, "Perception of Speech," Chapter 26 in *Handbook of Experimental Psychology*, ed. S. S. Stevens (New York: John Wiley & Sons, Inc., 1953), p. 1056.

[29] *Ibid.*, p. 1048.

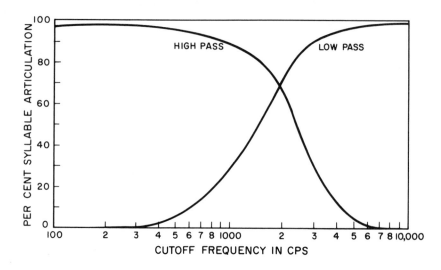

FIGURE 11. *Relationship of syllable articulation to frequency. (From S. S. Stevens, Handbook of Experimental Psychology, p. 1056.)*

capped person to determine his level of performance in perception of speech. They are:

(1) Speech detection threshold

(2) Speech reception threshold in quiet

(3) Speech reception threshold in noise

(4) Speech discrimination score

(5) Most comfortable listening range

(6) Tolerance threshold for speech

(7) Dynamic range

SPEECH DETECTION THRESHOLD

This is a measure of the listener's ability to determine the presence or absence of continuous speech. He merely indicates when he is aware that speech is being delivered to the sound field of the testing room. It is not necessary that he understand what is being said. This threshold provides the examiner with a basic measure of the level at which speech is detected 50 per cent of the time. The test material frequently employed is a calibrated recording of a nationally known news commentator.

SPEECH RECEPTION THRESHOLD IN QUIET

This threshold is a measure of the listener's ability to repeat correctly 50 per cent of the words that have been presented, either through phones or to the sound field. The threshold obtained compares favorably with the average of the threshold for detection of pure tones 500 cps, 1000 cps, and 2000 cps. The test material consists of selected words with spondaic stress pattern that were originally developed at Harvard but restructured for clinical use at the Central Institute for the Deaf by Hirsh and others.[30] (See Appendix.)

SPEECH RECEPTION THRESHOLD IN NOISE

This is a measure of the ability to hear in a background of competing noise. The materials utilized are the same as those for determining a speech reception threshold in quiet. The spondees are presented at a level of 20 db above the listener's speech reception threshold in quiet. Then white noise is delivered to the sound field as a distracting and competing signal. The level is increased from below threshold to a level at which the listener is repeating 50 per cent of the words correctly. If, for example, the level of the words being heard is 40 db and the level at which the noise causes 50 per cent error is 45 db, the ratio of the speech signal to the noise is 40 db/45 db. The resulting signal to noise score is −5 db, which means that the listener is capable of making 50 per cent correct identification of speech as it is immersed in noise that is 5 db more intense than the speech.

SPEECH DISCRIMINATION SCORE

This score indicates the discrimination loss for speech. The listener's task is to repeat monosyllables presented "at a level that is sufficiently high so that a further increase in intensity is not accompanied by a further increase in the amount of speech material repeated correctly."[31] Fifty words comprise the test and the performance is stated in terms of percentage of correct responses. (See Appendix, pp. 143–44.)

MOST COMFORTABLE LOUDNESS

Rather than being a point this is usually a range, at which continuous speech delivered to the sound field is heard and understood with ease. The range may vary in intensity as much as 10–20 db. for those with normal hearing. Material suitable for testing the most comfortable loudness (MCL), or perhaps more properly called the most comfortable loudness range (MCLR), is the same as for testing the detection threshold.

TOLERANCE THRESHOLD FOR SPEECH

This is, as the heading implies, the intensity level at which continuous speech delivered to the sound field of the listener is judged 50 per cent

[30] I. J. Hirsh, *et al.*, "Development of Materials for Speech Audiometry," *The Journal of Speech and Hearing Disorders* (1952), 17:321–37.
[31] *Ibid.*, p. 328.

of the time as being uncomfortably loud. Normal hearing subjects can usually tolerate up to 120 db (re: 0.0002 dyne/microbar). Frequently, those with sensorineural loss that is characterized by recruitment will tolerate far less intensity.

DYNAMIC RANGE

The dynamic range is the range of intensity that exists between the listener's speech reception threshold and his tolerance threshold for speech. This range indicates the useful auditory range for speech and is very meaningful to one administering auditory training. It is also of real significance to the audiologist as he makes recommendations concerning hearing aids.

The measures listed above are basic to the understanding of the perception of speech. However, they do not comprise the only important measures. Measures of the auditory perception of speech in the presence of visual distraction, visual cues augmenting the auditory perception of speech, general language development as it relates to the auditory perception of speech, and so forth, may also be helpful in developing a better understanding of the speech perception problems of the person with hearing loss.

SUMMARY

This chapter provides information concerning the nature of the perceptual process. It has been shown that perception has been defined differently by those who have been engaged in studying the problem. It is defined by various individuals with reference to their particular orientations. The neurophysiologist's definition will be in terms of neurophysiology and subsequent observable behaviors, whereas the psychologist with the gestalt viewpoint will interpret observations in the light of his molar orientation, and so forth.

Information was provided that dealt with audition in relation to the basic attributes of sound, such as intensity, frequency, and time, and the interrelationships that exist among them. Following the discussion on discrimination, a section was devoted to the topic of sound identification to emphasize the fact that sound discrimination can occur without the determination of the origin of the sound.

The final portion of the chapter dealt with those factors imoprtant to the perception of speech. Tests were suggested that are basic to the assessment of the perception of speech.

5

AUDITORY TRAINING FOR THE HEARING HANDI-
capped is a process by which the hard-of-hearing
individual learns to make maximum use of residual
hearing. There is a question about whether or not
residual hearing can be made more functional
through training. Excellent clinical evidence is
available in almost any program of aural rehabilitation to support the idea that auditory training is
worthwhile. Far less evidence is available that is
based on experimental study. Another question
concerns the selection of cases for auditory training. Auditory training is practicable only after it
has been determined, through otological inspection, that the hearing loss cannot be reversed by
medical or surgical procedures. Such training is

IMPORTANT
FACTORS
IN
AUDITORY TRAINING

necessary if the person sustaining the loss is handicapped in speech perception and/or speech intelligibility. Frequently it is indicated as a preventive measure for speech conservation. The discussion of any rationale of auditory training is based on principles of learning. For if it is auditory training that is provided, it can be explained within a learning-theory framework.

There is abundant information concerning the function of the normal ear, and more and more scientific evidence is being gathered on the performance of pathological ears. Volumes of material are available dealing with human learning. However, there is insufficient scientific evidence concerning the change in performance following the administration of auditory training procedures. Therefore at the present stage of development, it is virtually impossible to attempt to predict the actual behavior of the hearing handicapped after any specific set of procedures used in auditory training has been administered.

The purpose of this chapter is (1) to develop a concept of training within the framework of data available in the field of human learning, (2) to view some findings of auditory training research, and (3) to indicate some aspects of auditory training that need investigation.

THE CONCEPT OF TRAINING

The task involved in auditory training is similar to other training tasks designed to establish or improve a skill or set of skills. Factors influencing the effectiveness of training are many. One of the most important criteria by which to judge the effectiveness of auditory skills training for the hearing handicapped is that of speech perception. Self-adjustment and social adjustment to the handicap are important; however, speech perception improvement and an increased subsequent success in communication are closely intertwined with self-adjustment and social adjustment.

Auditory training or any skill training involves systematized and directed practice. What a hearing-handicapped person learns through periods of auditory training is partly attributable to the length of time he practices and the knowledge and competence of the audiologist who has outlined and is managing the aural rehabilitation program. Just as important to the success of auditory training are such factors as (1) motivation of the hearing-handicapped person, (2) intelligent cooperation with the clinician of those in close association with the hearing-handicapped individual, (3) age of the client, (4) intelligence of the client, (5) practice materials employed by the clinician, (6) opportunity for the client to have systematic practice, (7) establishment of proper habits by the client, (8) client's understanding of basic principles involved, (9) appropriateness of methods employed by the clinician, and (10) knowledge of progress.

MOTIVATION

Some who come to the auditory training situation are highly motivated and eager to begin training, whereas others have only moderate enthusiasm. Others passively accept the training because it has been prescribed for them. Still others become involved in training who are resistant to the whole idea of aural rehabilitation but have been persuaded to do something about their hearing problem by a wife, husband, or perhaps employer. Certainly any progress will depend in large measure on the degree of willingness to accept auditory training as an important and worthwhile undertaking. This does not mean, however, that the highly motivated, hard-of-hearing person will show tremendous progress and one with low motivation will make no progress. The other nine factors which have been listed are also important.

The writer has seen some hard-of-hearing persons show increased motivation when they are placed in competitive situations. This is one advantage of group therapy. In 1925 Hurlock[1] determined that praise improved performance levels. In 1928 Sims[2] showed how individual rivalry is a motivating force, more so than rivalry between groups. The point is that even though motivation may be lower than desirable, there are ways by which it can be increased. It is extremely difficult to administer auditory training or other aspects of aural rehabilitation to a person who lacks interest.

INTELLIGENT COOPERATION WITH THE CLINICIAN OF THOSE IN CLOSE ASSOCIATION WITH THE HEARING-HANDICAPPED INDIVIDUAL

The influence of others on the attitude of the hearing handicapped toward his problem should not be underestimated. It is not unusual for those who associate closely with the hearing handicapped to expect to see rapid progress made in the program of aural rehabilitation. If progress is not as rapid as expected, their disappointment is frequently obvious to the handicapped person, who in turn becomes discouraged.

It is of utmost importance that a realistic set of goals be outlined and understood by those who are near the person with hearing loss,

[1] E. B. Hurlock, "An Evaluation of Certain Incentives Used in Schoolwork," *Journal of Educational Psychology* (1925), 16:145–49.
[2] V. M. Sims. "The Relative Improvement of Two Types of Motivation on Improvement," *Journal of Educational Psychology* (1928), 19:480–84.

as well as by the handicapped individual. If this is accomplished and if those closest to the handicapped person are kept informed of the aims of the program as it progresses, much good can result. Those who live with the handicapped person can provide the opportunity for continued practice in the home and continued encouragement. Encouragement and understanding by others do not guarantee that the hearing-handicapped individual will maintain or increase his high level of motivation, but they provide the kind of support that frequently determines whether or not an attempt at aural rehabilitation is successful. Time devoted to counseling the family of the hard-of-hearing person serves a valuable purpose.

AGE OF THE CLIENT

Auditory training should be undertaken as soon as it is discovered that the hearing handicap cannot be reversed by medical or surgical intervention. This means that some youngsters who are one year old or even younger should receive training. At these early ages, habits of attending to sound are formed which are essential to later training involving discrimination among sounds. The Ewings[3] advocate starting auditory training as early as possible. Others who support this concept of early training are Wedenberg[4, 5] of Sweden and Frey and Whetnal[6] of England. It is particularly important because it affects early oral language development.

It is difficult to say much that is meaningful about chronological age and its importance as a factor in auditory training. In other learning tasks the evidence indicates a decrement in accuracy and extent of learning as the individual progresses from maturity to "old" age. When they have reached fifty, some persons are quite old and have literally "tuned out" the activities about them, whereas at eighty others are still intensely interested in life and wish to participate as fully as possible. Active involvement in the activities around one or the desire for more success in activities dependent on successful communications are far more useful than chronological age as criteria in deciding if auditory training is feasible for one of advanced years. It must be remembered, however, that a successful program of aural rehabilitation frequently

3 I. R. Ewing and A. W. G. Ewing, *Speech and the Deaf Child* (Washington, D.C.: The Volta Bureau, 1954).

4 E. Wedenberg, "Auditory Training of Deaf and Hard of Hearing Children," *Acta Otolaryngologica,* Supplement 94 (1950).

5 E. Wedenberg, "Auditory Training of Severely Hard of Hearing School Children," *Acta Otolaryngologica,* Supplement 110 (1954), 1–82.

6 D. B. Frey and E. Whetnal, "The Auditory Approach in Training Deaf Children", *Lancet* (1954), 266:584–87.

causes one who has lost interest in situations that call for speaking and hearing to regain that interest as an active participant.

INTELLIGENCE OF THE CLIENT

The determination of the lower limit, below which auditory training would not be possible, has not been established. There are no magic I.Q. or M.A. scores from which one can predict success or failure. It seems reasonable that the trainable mentally retarded person, whose capabilities enable him to care for himself and become economically useful in sheltered situations, could profit from auditory training. For, as Kirk[7] suggests, he is capable of learning some tasks. Kirk states, however, that "his speech and language will be distinctly limited." Although no experimental evidence is available, it would seem that the mentally retarded individual who is totally dependent could profit little, if any, from auditory training.

PRACTICE MATERIALS EMPLOYED BY THE CLINICIAN

The practice materials suggested for auditory training are comprised of an aggregate of sounds, noises, and speech. As one reviews the materials offered by numerous workers, it soon becomes evident that some have suggested, in a very casual way, the types of materials that can be useful. Others have constructed lists of various kinds of stimuli and suggest that there is an order to follow. Still others have systematically tried to structure activities that utilize particular sounds in specific ways. (Chapter 12 reviews auditory training materials.)

From the standpoint of good training, practice materials should be varied in many dimensions. A broad range of practice material will provide exposure that is comparable to the many situations in which the training will later be applied. This does not imply that there is no discrimination in the selection of material, but that there is a wide variety of stimulus conditions in which appropriate materials can be utilized. It is of particular importance in auditory training, where discrimination and identification are the objectives, that stimulus presentation is varied. In this way, learning to recognize the stimulus only when presented in a certain order will be avoided.

It has been demonstrated, however, that variation in practice material does decrease the speed of learning. Wolfle[8] has shown that as variation

[7] S. A. Kirk, M. B. Karnes, and W. D. Kirk, *You and Your Retarded Child* (New York: The Macmillan Company, 1958), p. 10.

[8] D. Wolfle, "The Relative Efficiency of Constant and Varied Stimulation During Learning," *Journal of Comparative Psychology* (1935), 19:5–27.

of the practice materials increases, the speed of learning decreases regularly.

OPPORTUNITY FOR THE CLIENT TO HAVE SYSTEMATIC PRACTICE

Regular practice of auditory training tasks is more beneficial than irregular and sporadic attempts. The real question is whether or not the material that is being practiced should be studied relatively continuously or in a series of short, auditory training sessions. The early findings of Ebbinghaus[9] would favor spacing out rather than concentrating the practice.

There are some arguments, however, for massing of effort. Hovland[10] suggests that in a massed effort the warm-up time is not as much of a problem as it is when the practice is distributed. Warm-up refers to the "getting set," as it were, when one undertakes a task. Much effort is expended in "warm-up" as one attempts, for example, to complete a term paper in three weeks when it is possible to spend only an hour or so each day at the task. The forgetting that occurs between periods of practice also favors massed practice.

A factor in favor of regularized distribution of practice periods in auditory training is that it prevents fatigue or boredom. It is important to combat monotony, and some of the exercises in auditory training can be somewhat monotonous and boring if prolonged. Another factor favoring distribution of practice is that of motivation. When a hard-of-hearing person remains too long at an auditory training task, his motivation frequently begins to decrease. Certain data from experimentation in human learning indicate that success can occur in a learning task, such as involved in auditory training, if the rehabilitation effort is concentrated. There is more convincing evidence, however, that adequate spacing of practice periods yields even better results.

STABLISHMENT OF PROPER HABITS BY THE CLIENT

To insure effective auditory training, the audiologist must make certain that the client develops certain habits that will increase his chances for success. Two items are of particular importance: (1) The hard-of-hearing person must develop the habit of listening carefully to instructions given at the outset of each exercise and of asking for further explanation

---

[9] Carl I. Hovland, "Human Learning and Retention," Chapter 17 in *Handbook of Experimental Psychology*, ed. S. S. Stevens (New York: John Wiley & Sons, 1953), p. 636.

[10] *Ibid.*, p. 638.

if he is not sure he has understood. (2) The hard-of-hearing person must be encouraged to check on the accuracy of his responses after each set of exercises.

CLIENT'S UNDERSTANDING OF BASIC PRINCIPLES INVOLVED

An important factor in learning is understanding the principles that support the task being performed. The audiologist should inform the handicapped individual, when possible, of the reasons for doing the tasks and of their underlying principles. These explanations should be simple enough to be clear and understandable to the handicapped person. An understanding of the general principles will enable the handicapped person to apply them to new tasks that have characteristics in common with the old.

APPROPRIATENESS OF METHODS EMPLOYED BY THE CLINICIAN

As is true in any other teaching-learning situation, good judgment must be exercised in selecting methods for presenting the practice materials in the auditory training period. Although no well-defined methods are established, some approaches have been found suitable for children and adults. With children the approach is often within the framework of a game, whereas with adults the method is geared to the appropriate level. A less objective or analytical approach is more often employed with children than with adults.

KNOWLEDGE OF PROGRESS

The literature on the psychology of learning generally is agreed that giving an immediate report of results to the subject after he has completed his task is of the utmost importance. The report should be as specific and complete as possible and should not indicate merely whether the trial was right or wrong. For example, if the hearing-handicapped person was listening to the number "fifteen" being spoken in the presence of noise and his reply was "sixteen," he should be made aware that the spoken number "fifteen" was the stimulus rather than merely being told that he had made a wrong judgment.

The ten factors mentioned above are important to consider as one attempts to develop a concept of training that is relevant to the problem of auditory training for the hard of hearing.

SOME AUDITORY TRAINING RESEARCH FINDINGS

Ever since society has shown concern in assisting its acoustically handicapped members, there has been some interest in increasing the usefulness of hearing through training of one kind or another. Certain questions have occurred to those involved in devising such training: How severely hard of hearing must one be before he cannot benefit from training aimed at increasing the usefulness of residual hearing? What procedures should be employed in auditory training? How shall the success of the procedures be measured? What considerations should be given to the use of the visual channel as an adjunct to auditory training? What is the value of the hearing aid in aural rehabilitation? Answers to some of these questions have been found.

Early in the nineteenth century, Itard experimented with blindfolded deaf persons and discovered that repeated sound stimulation produced noticeable increase in response. He then proceeded to develop a training approach to be used with the hearing handicapped. Later in the nineteenth century, Urbantschitsch and also Bell made some systematic observations of the effects of auditory training. Goldstein made some of the most profound contributions to the development of auditory training in America and published his approach and observations in his text, *Acoustic Method*.[11]

At various times, from the turn of the twentieth century until the present, investigators have reported results of research in auditory training. Many of the results are somewhat tenuous and inconclusive. Urbantschitsch[12] in 1904 suggested that it was difficult to predict success in auditory training because of the effects of mental attitudes and capacities. Forrester[13] showed that, following a year of auditory training, approximately 50 per cent of the students revealed no appreciable change in their hearing status, whereas 40 per cent revealed a 5-db shift in one ear and 12 per cent showed a noticeable loss of acuity.

In her attempt to determine the results of auditory training, Johnson[14] studied the effects of training on students at the Illinois School for the Deaf. She reported on the retention of vocabulary and stated that her students retained over 80 per cent of the drill vocabulary. Later studies

[11] M. Goldstein, *The Acoustic Method for the Training of the Deaf and Hard of Hearing Child* (St. Louis: Laryngoscope Press, 1939), p. 246.
[12] V. Urbantschitsch, "On the Value of Methodological Exercises in Hearing," *The Association Review* (1904), 6:48–52.
[13] C. R. Forrester, "Residual Hearing and Its Bearing on Oral Training," *American Annals of the Deaf* (1928), 23:147–55.
[14] E. H. Johnson, "Testing Results of Acoustic Training," *American Annals of the Deaf* (1939), 84:223–33.

were somewhat more objective and better controlled. Di Carlo[15] has shown that adults with hearing loss can profit greatly from auditory training after having been fitted with hearing aids. Silverman[16] has demonstrated that the tolerance thresholds for discomfort, tickle, and pain can be extended through training with both normal and hard-of-hearing individuals.

It has been shown through investigation that persons suffering from losses averaging 40 db or less can profit from auditory training without the help of a hearing aid, whereas those with greater losses profit more when training is given with a hearing aid.[17] Comparisons have been made of the results of auditory training given to children who were deaf and children considered hard of hearing. After a four-year study, Wedenberg[18] concluded that those who were deaf showed actual progress in hearing. Over 50 per cent of the hard-of-hearing children did show significant improvement.

Some of the greatest contributions to research in the area of auditory training were made by Hudgins and his colleagues at the Clarke School for the Deaf. Hudgins[19] was a firm proponent of the multisensory approach in aural rehabilitation of the acoustically handicapped. He[20] suggested that there are three thresholds of importance: (1) detection, (2) tolerance, and (3) speech perception. His research efforts were directed toward exploration of these thresholds as they were affected by auditory training. In one study he showed that children with average losses of 80 db and greater can benefit in speech perception, speech intelligibility, speech phrasing, and educational achievement as they are given auditory training with powerful hearing aids.[21]

In a study aimed at determining the relationship between the degree of deafness and response to auditory training, Hopkins and Hudgins[22] found that there is a wide variation among deaf children in their response to training. It appeared that the variability noted was not meaningfully

[15] L. Di Carlo, "Auditory Training for the Adult," *The Volta Review* (1948), 490–96.

[16] S. R. Silverman, "Tolerance for Pure Tones and Speech in Normal and Defective Hearing," *Annals of Otology, Rhinology, and Laryngology* (1947), 56:658–77.

[17] V. L. Browd, "Hearing Re-education Without the Use of Hearing Aids," *Archives of Otolaryngology* (1949), 49:511–28.

[18] E. Wedenberg, "Auditory Training of Deaf and Hard of Hearing Children," *Acta Otolaryngologica* (1951), 94:130 pages.

[19] C. V. Hudgins, "Problems of Speech Comprehension in Deaf Children," *The Nervous Child* (1951), 9:57–63.

[20] C. V. Hudgins, "A Rationale for Acoustic Training," *The Volta Review* (1948), 50:484–90.

[21] C. V. Hudgins. "The Response of Profoundly Deaf Children to Auditory Training," *Journal of Speech and Hearing Disorders* (1953), 18:273–88.

[22] L. A. Hopkins and C. V. Hudgins, "The Relationship Between Degree of Deafness and Response to Acoustic Training," *The Volta Review* (1953), 55:32–35.

related to severity of hearing loss or to the extent of the frequency range involved. They concluded that all deaf children should be given opportunity to develop their residual hearing. In an address before the Alexander Graham Bell Association for the Deaf in 1954, Hudgins[23] presented data which vividly portrayed the gains that can be made through a bisensory (eye-ear) approach to aural rehabilitation. Following auditory training his students showed improvement in speech perception, speech intelligibility, and positive acceleration in educational progress.

Quick[24] contributed a test for measuring the speech perception of young deaf children. The vocabulary was based on the first-and second-year vocabulary lists of the Primary Department of the Clarke School for the Deaf. The tests yield some valid and reliable results in measuring speech perception of young acoustically handicapped children.[25]

In 1954 Di Carlo[26] reviewed some of the research trends in aural rehabilitation and suggested that the use of hearing aids may be beneficial to deaf children, but that they were even more beneficial to children with 60 db or less loss, depending on when the aid was provided and the amount and type of auditory training the children received. Strizver[27] in 1958 hypothesized that pupils achieving high scores in performance on speech perception tests should also be more successful in recognizing differences in pitch. His results with twenty pupils of Clarke school indicated, among other things, that there was no significant correlation between speech perception and frequency discrimination within the 1000-cps and 2000-cps range. He suggests that the variability in success in auditory training may be due to pitch-discrimination ability at low frequencies and hearing acuity for high frequencies.

NEED FOR CONTINUED RESEARCH

Even though some fine work has been accomplished in research on auditory training, results are fragmentary and inconclusive. It would seem profitable, for purposes of rehabilitation, to determine the ways

[23] C. V. Hudgins, "Auditory Training: Its Possibilities and Limitations," *The Volta Bureau* (1954), 11 pages.

[24] M. A. Quick, "A Test for Measuring Achievement in Speech Perception Among Young Deaf Children" (Unpublished M.A. Thesis, Department of Education, Smith College, 1952).

[25] A brief account of the test development is presented in the following: C. V. Hudgins *et al.*, "Speech and Speech Perception," *The Volta Review* (1953), 53:10–13.

[26] L. M. Di Carlo, "Research Trends and Practical Applications," *The Volta Review* (1954), 56:351–53.

[27] G. L. Strizver, "Frequency Discrimination of Deaf Children and Its Relationship to Their Achievement in Auditory Training," *The Volta Review* (1958), 60:304–6.

in which sounds are distorted, as a function of type and severity of hearing loss. The next step would be to relate this information to performance in tasks involving auditory perception. With this information, one would be in a position to construct not only additional tests of diagnostic value but also materials and approaches based on scientific evidence of what was needed for the rehabilitation process. Although there seems to be no question about the merit of the multisensory approach in aural rehabilitation, two areas that are in need of further research are cutaneous perception of sound pressure and its relationship to auditory perception.

SUMMARY

The material in this chapter was presented to help the student see some of the important factors in auditory training. Specifically, the aim was to assist the reader in the development of a rationale for auditory training that relates meaningfully to the facts available concerning human learning. Secondly, an attempt was made to present some of the research efforts directed toward measurement of auditory training. Finally, several suggestions were made for further research pertinent to aural rehabilitation.

6

CHILDREN WHO HEAR NORMALLY DEVELOP ORAL language because of the auditory stimulation they receive from parents, siblings, and others in their environment. The child who is hard of hearing is deprived of a part of this stimulation; therefore, the development of his oral language suffers at both receptive and expressive levels. To understand the importance of auditory training for the hearing-handicapped child who is impaired in oral language, it is necessary to examine carefully the normal patterns of language development.

A child passes through well-defined stages in the development of functional oral language. Although these have been outlined by numerous writers, they are closely related to this subject

AUDITORY TRAINING AND ORAL LANGUAGE DEVELOPMENT

matter and will therefore be reviewed. Just as children develop at different rates with respect to walking, self-feeding, and other activities involving motor coordination, so do they differ in the mastery of oral language. Ages and stages that are mentioned in discussing oral language development pertain to the "average" child. Children of specific ages will be at certain stages of development.

Early workers in the field of child language frequently concentrated on one child's development and generalized from their observations. Later researchers had large groups of children available in research centers and nurseries and based their findings on the samples derived from many youngsters. Piaget, Baldwin, Stecher, McCarthy, Mowrer, and Templin[1] are most important in the early work on language development. Many others, too numerous to mention, have also made notable contribution to the literature.

AGES AND STAGES OF ORAL LANGUAGE DEVELOPMENT

BIRTH CRY AND SUBSEQUENT REFLEXIVE VOCALIZATION

If a newborn baby does not make himself known vocally, doubt arises about his health. However, if events occur normally, the infant will produce some rousing nasalized [æ] sounds. His first utterances do not result from being stimulated by acoustic events in his environment. His cry is simply reflexive. Thus, auditory training would not be possible or important at this stage of development. Furthermore, a deaf baby, who is normal in all other respects, would be expected to produce as vigorous a vocal output at birth as the infant who is born with no hearing deficit.

Following his birth, the baby continues to make himself known by his cries. In the first few weeks his cries are undifferentiated; however, after this period the careful observer can detect a difference in cries that are associated with a variety of sensations the infant experiences. The cries related to pressure, pain, heat or cold, hunger and thirst differ to some extent from each other. As yet, the vocal output is little affected by self-hearing or purely external acoustic events, but varies as a function of stimuli impinging upon sensory receptors, other than the auditory.

[1] Some key references associated with the names listed are: a. Jean Piaget, *The Language and Thought of the Child* (New York: Harcourt, Brace & World, Inc., 1926); b. B. T. Baldwin and L. I. Stecher, *Psychology of the Pre-school Child* (New York: Appleton-Century-Crofts, 1924; c. D. McCarthy, "Research in Language Development: Retrospect and Prospect," *Monograph of the Society for Research in Child Development* (1959), 24:3–24; d. H. O. Mowrer, "Speech Development in the Young Child," *Journal of Speech and Hearing Disorders* (1952), 17:263–68; e. M. Templin, "Certain Language Skills in Children, Their Development and Interrelationship," *University of Minnesota Institute of Child Welfare Monograph Series* (1957), No. 26.

BABBLING

The next noticeable level of development is that of babbling. This stage begins any time from the fifth to the eighth week of life. During this stage the baby is producing many sounds he will use later and some that he will eventually discard because they are not part of the language he will learn. Sound combinations like ba–ba–ba, da–da–da, uhbuh, bidduh, and many, many more comprise the babbling vocabulary. The child with auditory impairment babbles just as do children with normal hearing; however, he does not continue to do so. Van Riper[2] suggests, however, that "deaf babies... soon lose interest, and teaching them to talk correctly is a very difficult task."

At the babbling stage of development the child begins to imitate his own vocal attempts in preparation for imitating those of others in his environment. At this point auditory stimulation, self-stimulation, makes a difference. It is logical that from this point the child who cannot hear normally can begin to profit from some auditory training that will be consistent with his level of development. He must develop with the understanding that the sounds he makes and the sounds others make are important. Babbling frequently continues into the echolalic period, during which the baby attempts to modify his sound output to imitate those he hears.

ECHOLALIA

This stage of development, occurring during the final quarter of the first year, frequently causes parents to become more aware of the emergence of speech than do any of the preceding stages. At this stage the child literally echos those sounds and sound combinations he has perfected and the language units he hears. It is not unusual for the proud parent to become quite elated as he hears his youngster utter some words that may be quite complex phonetically, even though the utterances have no meaning for the child.

During this time when the child is keenly aware of sounds, auditory training is important for the normal-hearing child, but particularly for the child who appears to sustain a decreased hearing level.

WORDS

Most children will utter actual words between the ages of one and one-and-a-half years. It is not unusual, however, for an intelligent child to listen for a longer period before trying to communicate with

---

[2] C. Van Riper, *Teaching Your Child to Talk* (New York: Harper and Row, Publishers, Inc., 1950), p. 18.

established word units. It is difficult to tell "when a word becomes a word." How does one differentiate between "real words" and mere sound combinations that have all the acoustic characteristics of words? "Real words" for children at a receptive level are those that cause a desired response. As the desired response takes place, we believe the child has understood and thus has dealt meaningfully with a word that is "real" to him at his level of reception.

Utilization of "real words" at the receptive level precedes the use of "real words" at the level of expression. To say that a child has used "real words" at the level of expression means that there is sufficient evidence from the child's behavior and the context in which the word is used to indicate that he has attempted to evoke meaning via oral language.

It is of particular importance at this stage of development that good auditory training be provided. In most instances this occurs quite naturally as interested parents and siblings talk to the baby. However, the aurally handicapped child needs extra help and care. Early planning and training can prove tremendously valuable as the child builds a vocabulary. Of course, early, specialized auditory training depends on early detection of hearing loss.

AGE LEVELS OF SPEECH SOUND MASTERY AND USAGE OF VARIOUS PARTS OF SPEECH

To determine whether or not a child is slow in developing the sounds of speech and the words of the language, one must view the development against a set of norms or standards.

SPEECH SOUND DEVELOPMENT

Table II presents data gathered by Poole[3] and illustrates that the plosives develop before the more complicated fricatives. The table is presented as just one source of data. Still another set of data, including

TABLE II.

Age in Years	Sounds Mastered						
3½	[b],	[p],	[m],	[w],	[h],		
4½	[d],	[t],	[n],	[g],	[k],	[ŋ],	[j],
5½	[f]						
6½	[v],	[ð],	[ʒ],	[ʃ],	[l],		
7½	[s],	[z],	[r],	[θ],	[hw]		

3 I. Poole, "Genetic Development of Articulation of Consonant Sounds in Speech," *Elementary English Review* (1934), 2:159–61.

TABLE III. Vowel And Consonant Phoneme Percentages

	Age, months															
	2	4	6	8	10	12	14	16	18	20	22	24	26	28	30	Adult
	Number of infants															
	62	80	75	64	62	62	57	55	50	41	37	31	32	24	19	
i	0.14	1.10	1.77	1.80	2.09	4.15	4.32	6.62	7.05	7.63	9.71	11.42	11.63	12.16	13.44	7.40
I	27.39	21.89	24.82	24.96	22.22	23.02	23.13	24.96	22.46	20.61	17.27	19.22	18.42	21.07	18.38	20.56
e	0.16	1.08	1.58	2.04	2.85	3.25	3.25	3.24	3.07	3.01	2.64	3.11	4.20	2.54	2.70	5.21
ɛ	42.98	33.91	31.27	31.40	32.35	27.56	27.03	22.00	18.17	14.34	12.51	12.19	8.72	8.94	7.48	7.98
æ	1.82	2.65	2.62	3.13	2.72	4.13	2.25	2.97	3.22	3.83	3.85	4.38	4.30	4.89	4.63	8.06
ʌ	25.18	25.56	23.44	19.65	16.80	16.17	16.58	15.13	15.73	16.16	14.65	13.15	13.58	12.63	13.43	1.12
ə	—	0.23	0.25	0.15	0.18	0.20	0.40	0.80	0.77	1.03	1.55	1.02	1.04	1.95	3.24	17.76
ɑ	0.21	2.18	1.52	2.17	5.34	6.48	6.64	6.58	8.37	10.98	11.73	13.09	13.43	14.95	13.67	10.85
ɔ	—	0.10	0.20	0.22	0.47	0.64	0.80	0.67	1.61	1.63	2.30	3.08	2.27	1.52	2.54	5.58
o	—	0.18	0.17	0.30	0.68	1.33	1.17	2.25	3.76	3.08	5.29	4.54	6.58	5.27	6.74	5.54
U	1.75	7.70	8.20	10.12	10.24	7.71	8.79	8.88	10.44	11.57	10.97	10.27	10.59	9.42	9.51	4.60
u	0.31	3.41	4.17	3.88	4.06	5.36	5.69	5.92	5.32	6.10	7.49	4.50	5.24	4.58	4.19	5.21

	Age, months															Adult
	2	4	6	8	10	12	14	16	18	20	22	24	26	28	30	
p	0.10	0.20	0.30	1.13	0.67	1.63	1.07	2.10	1.27	2.73	4.17	4.32	3.57	3.63	4.47	2.41
b	0.19	1.54	2.50	4.47	7.97	9.79	9.48	11.95	14.95	13.38	13.52	8.97	8.81	7.34	7.64	3.18
m	0.21	0.66	3.07	5.21	7.53	6.69	9.23	5.74	5.43	7.38	8.45	8.41	7.14	7.29	7.99	4.47
w	0.07	1.10	1.49	0.96	2.64	3.31	4.36	4.55	7.02	4.61	5.19	6.42	5.77	3.83	3.31	2.99
hw	—	—	—	—	0.02	0.08	0.34	0.05	0.04	0.15	0.20	0.03	0.21	0.11	0.20	0.60
f	—	0.16	0.27	0.56	0.73	0.37	0.45	0.47	0.63	0.81	1.37	1.13	2.19	1.73	1.79	3.48
v	—	0.40	0.16	0.90	1.22	1.03	0.44	0.42	0.29	0.49	0.29	0.52	0.68	0.57	0.63	2.52
θ	—	0.37	0.39	0.49	1.49	0.85	0.67	0.38	0.29	0.36	0.11	0.36	—	0.06	0.14	1.06
ð	0.17	0.39	0.34	0.30	0.17	0.34	0.43	0.30	0.36	0.56	0.61	0.61	0.68	0.62	1.70	5.13
t	—	—	0.22	1.05	1.68	4.34	3.96	4.14	4.61	5.57	7.43	8.31	10.12	11.17	11.68	11.66
d	—	2.64	2.06	6.46	15.73	20.58	19.42	20.04	20.56	18.45	15.07	15.31	14.25	16.20	13.98	8.28
n	0.14	0.35	0.52	1.68	1.03	2.65	2.07	3.11	5.38	7.89	8.85	9.74	9.31	10.07	9.49	11.85
s	—	0.05	0.20	0.17	1.65	3.45	2.81	3.08	3.59	3.51	6.06	7.42	7.98	8.11	6.87	7.54
z	—	0.07	—	0.12	0.21	0.56	0.69	1.23	1.00	1.14	0.65	0.51	0.58	0.23	0.41	3.48
ʃ	—	0.09	0.02	—	0.33	0.37	0.25	0.29	0.41	0.50	1.08	0.84	1.40	0.93	0.82	1.64
ʒ	—	—	—	—	—	0.10	—	0.02	0.11	0.04	0.07	0.09	0.07	—	—	0.67
l	0.21	0.99	0.23	0.12	1.37	0.96	0.57	1.57	1.04	1.47	1.93	2.08	2.51	3.06	3.37	6.32
r	—	—	0.15	0.51	—	0.10	0.18	0.53	1.09	0.99	1.54	2.67	3.96	4.12	4.64	10.51
j	—	0.72	1.12	1.14	2.15	1.77	3.78	2.29	1.95	2.80	1.64	1.73	1.69	2.04	1.50	1.89
ç	—	0.09	—	0.06	0.16	0.06	0.11	0.29	—	0.02	—	—	0.06	0.09	0.10	—
ŋ	—	0.26	0.17	0.80	0.03	0.33	0.31	0.03	0.14	0.42	0.31	0.62	0.84	0.99	0.48	1.68
k	8.80	2.78	4.90	2.05	1.82	2.12	2.36	2.76	2.73	4.04	6.04	4.36	6.74	6.16	6.98	4.15
g	2.79	11.73	7.46	5.43	4.12	4.15	4.91	5.55	5.17	4.46	4.47	2.67	3.33	3.18	4.05	1.75
x	—	0.04	0.10	0.01	0.14	0.08	0.05	—	0.02	0.09	0.04	—	0.07	0.03	—	—
h	44.22	59.88	61.93	57.87	41.29	31.77	29.75	26.69	20.75	16.29	9.84	10.93	7.53	8.14	7.65	2.66
ʔ	42.91	15.48	12.41	8.51	5.84	2.52	2.31	2.19	1.12	1.85	1.07	1.90	0.44	0.22	0.07	—

TABLE IV. *Mean Per Cent of Each Part of Speech by Age and Sex**
(Based on total number of words used)

Age in Months	Sex	Nouns	Verbs	Adjec.	Adv.	Pronouns	Con-junc.	Prep.	Int.	Misc.
18	B	43.6	16.7	5.1	5.1	12.8	0.0	0.0	16.7	0.0
	G	51.5	13.1	10.7	8.5	9.8	0.6	0.0	5.5	0.3
	All	50.0	13.9	9.4	7.9	10.3	0.3	0.0	7.6	0.3
24	B	49.3	15.3	5.8	3.7	15.4	0.0	2.0	3.4	5.4
	G	35.5	22.6	11.6	8.0	14.5	0.7	4.1	2.2	0.8
	All	38.6	21.0	10.3	7.1	14.6	0.5	3.6	2.4	1.8
30	B	25.4	24.9	14.4	6.3	21.0	0.5	4.3	1.5	1.8
	G	26.0	22.3	14.8	6.9	17.2	2.5	4.9	3.8	1.7
	All	25.8	23.4	14.3	6.7	19.0	1.7	4.6	2.8	1.8
36	B	23.6	23.5	15.4	6.8	21.3	1.1	5.4	1.5	0.6
	G	23.2	22.5	16.7	6.3	17.3	3.7	8.4	1.5	0.5
	All	23.4	23.0	16.1	7.0	19.2	2.4	6.9	1.5	0.5
42	B	12.5	25.3	15.1	8.4	19.7	3.0	6.7	2.4	1.0
	G	18.5	27.0	16.6	7.0	21.8	1.3	5.8	1.6	1.5
	All	18.5	26.0	15.7	7.8	20.3	2.3	6.3	2.0	0.8
48	B	19.7	26.8	13.7	6.7	20.5	3.3	7.3	0.9	1.0
	G	20.4	25.3	15.4	5.2	22.5	3.8	6.2	0.6	0.6
	All	20.1	26.0	14.6	5.9	21.6	3.6	6.7	0.8	0.8
54	B	19.4	25.0	14.4	7.7	21.1	4.0	6.7	0.9	0.9
	G	19.3	25.3	16.1	6.3	19.9	3.5	7.6	1.4	0.6
	All	19.3	25.1	15.2	7.0	20.5	3.8	7.1	1.2	0.8

the vowels and consonants, is presented in Table III, which shows the research of Irwin[4] done at the Iowa Child Welfare Research Station.

USAGE OF VARIOUS PARTS OF SPEECH

Table IV presents the results of McCarthy's study[5] on parts of speech used by children from 18 through 54 months of age. Various estimates of the total vocabulary of children have been made: 2 to 3 words at age one; 350–400 words at age two; and approximately 1000 words at age three.

EFFECTS OF HEARING LOSS ON LANGUAGE LEARNING

When impairment exists in any sensory input system, one can expect decreased function in proportion to the degree of deficit. Therefore, in

[4] O. Irwin, "Infant Speech: Consonantal Sounds According to Place of Articulation," *The Journal of Speech Disorders* (1947), 12:397–401; "Infant Speech: Consonant Sounds According to Manner of Articulation," *The Journal of Speech Disorders* (1947), 12:402–4; "Infant Speech: Development of Vowel Sounds," *The Journal of Speech and Hearing Disorders* (1948), 13:31–34.

[5] D. McCarthy, *Language Development of the Pre-school Child* (Minneapolis: The University of Minnesota Press, 1930), p. 114.

the case of decreased auditory sensitivity, one can expect that learning which is related to acoustic events will suffer in relation to the degree of hearing loss. Even though children who are diagnosed as deaf are found to have normal intelligence, as measured by such tests as the Nebraska Test of Learning Aptitude, the Grace Arthur Scale, the Wechsler Intelligence Scale for Children, and the Randall's Island Performance Series, they are frequently retarded two or more years in educational achievement.[6] Children who are not deaf, but hard of hearing, might be within the normal range intellectually and show retardation in educational achievement in proportion to the severity of their loss.

Since concept development is so intricately intertwined with language learning, one finds that the acoustically handicapped child is often behind the normal-hearing child in this respect. However, the degree to which any individual child who sustains a hearing loss will perform is dependent on numerous factors, among which are:

(1) Severity of the loss
(2) Age at onset of the loss
(3) Age at which the loss was detected
(4) Extent to which specialized training was provided
(5) Opportunity for educational experiences
(6) Opportunity for socialization

Although language learning occurs at a slower pace with the hard-of-hearing than with the normal-hearing child, it is much more difficult for the child who is deaf. Some workers suggest that even though a child has a loss as great as 60 decibels and does not learn language spontaneously he will have an advantage over the deaf child because of his auditory residual.[7] Amplified residual hearing, coupled with kinesthetic cues, provides valuable assistance in the reception and production of oral language.

TYPICAL SPEECH AND VOICE PATTERNS OF THE HARD OF HEARING

Just as a severe hearing loss can make a difference in educational achievement, so can it affect speech and voice production. The hard-of-hearing person fails to hear certain sounds or parts of sounds, and his voice and articulation reflect this fact. The nuances and subtleties of inflection, pitch, and loudness of voice, along with the fine variations

[6] S. Berlinsky, "Measurement of the Intelligence and Personality of the Deaf: A Review of the Literature," *Journal of Speech and Hearing Disorders* (1952), 17:39–55.

[7] A. Streng, W. J. Fitch, L. D. Hedgecock, J. W. Phillips, and J. A. Carrell, *Hearing Therapy for Children* (New York: Grune and Stratton, 1955), p. 179.

that occur in the production of consonants, are frequently not within the experience of the acoustically handicapped. Thus, a difference in speech and voice patterns of the hard of hearing is to be expected.

The ear serves as a monitor in the production of voice and articulation. This becomes evident when we increase the noise level in the speaker's ear and observe an increase in his vocal intensity or delay the auditory feedback of the speaker's voice and witness his nonfluent speech. Likewise, if the individual does not receive a part of the acoustic spectrum important to human speech, nasality, distorted vowels, and misarticulated consonants will be present in his speech.

A study made by Oyer and Doudna[8] of auditory discrimination performance of hard-of-hearing adults, who were diagnosed otologically as having "conductive" or "other than conductive" hearing losses proved the following facts pertinent.

(1) Sound substitutions occur more frequently in the discrimination task than do omissions and insertions.

(2) Confusions within groups of consonants are very similar for both hearing loss categories except for nasals and blends. It appears that somewhat less confusion in the nonconductive group occurs on blends, whereas somewhat more confusion occurs on the nasals.

(3) The PB words containing two, three, four, and five sounds showed no marked differences in intelligibility.

(4) Sound omissions and insertions in error responses occur most frequently in the final position of the word.

(5) Discrimination losses decrease when a task is presented a second time.

(6) Although vowel confusions occurred less frequently than did consonant confusions, a significantly greater proportion of confusions occurred among vowels than among consonants.

(7) There is a difference in the degree to which the subjects with conductive loss and those with nonconductive loss will perseverate in their error responses. Those with conductive loss were more consistent at each age level in repeating their errors than those with nonconductive loss.

These findings emphasize the fact that auditory discrimination problems differ somewhat as a function of the type of hearing loss. A worthwhile followup on this research would be one that focused on a phonetic analysis of the speech of the hard-of-hearing individuals in each of the two categories.

O'Neill[9] suggests that the presence of hearing loss does not necessarily mean that there will be voice or speech disturbances but will depend

---

[8] H. J. Oyer and M. Doudna, "Structural Analysis of Word Responses Made by Hard of Hearing Subjects on a Discrimination Test," *A.M.A. Archives of Otolaryngology* (1959), 70:357–64.

[9] J. J. O'Neill, *The Hard of Hearing* (Englewood Cliffs, N.J.: Prentice-Hall, Inc., 1964), p. 111.

on the extent of the loss, the patient's age, and the length of time he has had the loss. He emphasizes early detection and application of aural rehabilitation procedures. He suggests that there is still some real question about the effect hearing loss has on language learning, but indicates there may be some effects.

In a very detailed analysis of voice and speech patterns of the hard of hearing, Penn[10] found that there were some differences among the 100 adults who had perceptive losses and the 100 with conductive losses that he studied. He concluded that hearing defects are associated with voice and speech patterns and that the nature of the loss is important as it relates to the nature of the speech or voice anomaly. His analyses showed that there were differentiating characteristics of voice and speech for conductive and perceptive losses. Perceptive losses were associated most frequently with the following:

(1) Excessive volume
(2) Nasal quality
(3) Poor mobility of articulators
(4) Strident quality
(5) Monotonous pitch
(6) Rapid rate
(7) Audible breathing
(8) General vowel confusion
(9) Omission of high-frequency consonants in consonantal clusters
(10) Unconscious phonation
(11) Deviations of: [r], [e], [ð], [s] [l], [tʃ], [dʒ], [ʒ], [ʃ], and [ʒ]

In conductive type loss, the following characteristics were most frequently observed:

(1) Denasal quality
(2) Weak volume
(3) Unvoiced, weak, or omitted final consonants
(4) Deviations of: [m] [n]

In the case of conductive loss, the individual can still monitor his voice effectively as it passes through the tissue between the larynx and ear. That is, he hears and controls his body-conducted sidetone. The person with perceptive loss, however, cannot do this because of the nature of his loss. Actually, speech and voice aberrations are greater among the persons with hearing losses of a perceptive nature than of a conductive nature.

IMPORTANCE OF EARLY DETECTION OF HEARING LOSS

It is difficult to overemphasize the importance of early determination of a youngster's hearing status if a loss is suspected. Too often the

---

[10] J. P. Penn, "Voice and Speech Patterns of the Hard of Hearing," *Acta-Otolaryngologica,* Supplementum 124 (1955).

parents may realize that something is not right when their child does not start to talk. Too often they are told to stop worrying—everything will turn out all right. Happily, in some cases it does, but in others the outcome is not so good.

The writer has seen children who have adjusted so well to hearing loss that they have not been detected by either parents or teachers until they are into the third or fourth grades. By this time much valuable time has been lost, and the speech and language patterns are delayed. Of course, it avails little if a loss is detected early and a program of aural rehabilitation is not provided.

IMPORTANCE OF EARLY AURAL HABILITATION PROCEDURES

If otological inspection and audiological evaluation prove that a hearing aid should be fitted, the parents must understand the importance of amplification. Sometimes this is not difficult at all; however, in some instances the writer has had a difficult time convincing parents of very young children that a hearing aid is needed.

A child should be fitted with a hearing aid, just as soon as it is established that there is a loss of sufficient magnitude to warrant amplification. Another question arises about the age when the acoustically handicapped child should receive the benefit of auditory training. Audiologists do not all agree on the answer. This writer's experience indicates that a program of aural habilitation should be arranged for the child within the clinic when it is needed. This can be done in conjunction with a correspondence course such as is provided by the John Tracy Clinic of Los Angeles. Plans should be made in close cooperation with parents so that they develop an appreciation and understanding of what must be done to encourage good speech and language development. The earlier a child who has a hearing loss is provided with specialized help, the better.

SUMMARY

This chapter has emphasized the importance of auditory training for the hearing-handicapped child so that oral language development might take place. A review has been made of the various stages of language development the child passes through. A discussion of the effects of hearing loss on language learning was also presented. Degree of hearing loss is a salient factor in the learning of language. Children with slight loss may vary only slightly from children with normal hearing in producing the sounds of speech. Children with profund losses not only have difficulty in producing the phonetic elements, but in addition have real problems of a linguistic nature. Research shows that voice and speech patterns of the hard of hearing are different from those of persons who hear normally. The patterns vary according to the nature of the hearing loss.

7

COSTLY ELECTRONIC EQUIPMENT IS NOT IMPERA-tive, but it can be of great assistance in administering a program of auditory training. With it, one can control the sound pressure levels at which the sound used as training materials are presented. Furthermore, if the equipment has a filter network, one can present selected portions of the acoustic spectrum and thereby emphasize or deemphasize certain ranges as desired. In other words, with electronic equipment one can more effectively control the sounds that are employed in the auditory training of the hearing handicapped. In some settings, the more elaborate equipment is not available, and the clinician must depend on his own ingenuity in administering stimuli in the training

AUDITORY TRAINING EQUIPMENT

situation. However, more and more clinics and centers are acquiring electronic instruments that are especially designed for auditory training. In this case, the clinician must learn how to use the equipment to its best advantage.

Various kinds of instruments have been used in giving auditory stimuli to hearing-handicapped persons throughout the past. As early as the first century, the use of a hearing trumpet was advocated for stimulating the ear of the deaf. Loud noises were directed toward the trumpet and amplified by it. The hearing trumpet was used for many centuries. Bells, whistles, and a variety of musical instruments were used as sound sources to be directed to the ear via the trumpet. The advent of the vacuum tube, microphones, and electronic amplifiers rekindled the notion that sounds could be profitably provided to the deaf and hard of hearing. The advent of the electronic hearing aid in the 1920's also caused renewed effort by those involved in habilitation and rehabilitation programs for people with hearing deficits.

BASIC COMPONENTS OF AUDITORY TRAINING EQUIPMENT

The components of a commercial auditory training unit will vary depending on its cost. A relatively inexpensive unit probably will be less complex and thus less flexible. Before commercial units became so easily available, some clinics tried to construct, from their own store of components, sets that could be used in their auditory training program.

There are some basic requirements of auditory training equipment. It should have an input or microphone for picking up sounds. It must amplify the sounds after they have been fed to it through the microphone. Amplification must be controllable to regulate the intensity with which sounds are presented to the ears of the hearing handicapped. Next, the system should enable presentation of selected frequency segments of the sounds that the clinician wishes to employ in the training. In other words, it should provide a filter network. Lastly, there must be a means by which the sounds can then be made available to the person being trained. This can occur through a set or a series of sets of earphones, a loudspeaker or loudspeakers. A turntable for playing back recorded auditory training materials is very convenient. Figure

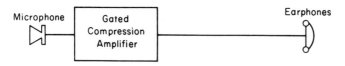

FIGURE 12. *Components of a simple auditory training unit.*

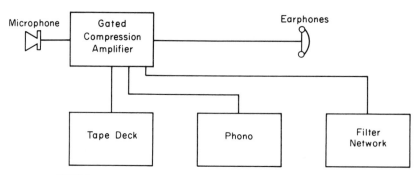

FIGURE 13. *Components of a more complex auditory training unit.*

12 is a schematic representation in block diagram of the basic components of an auditory training unit, and Figure 13 presents a schematic of a somewhat more complex unit.

GENERAL TYPES OF AUDITORY TRAINING EQUIPMENT EMPLOYED

The types of equipment employed in auditory training may be classified and described in many ways. One person may consider the equipment's usability with children or adults and another may be concerned with its cost. Or it may be classified in terms of the gain versus frequency characteristics. For our purposes here, equipment for auditory training is classified and described in terms of types that are available for use. Pictures and brief descriptions of some of the available equipment have been included. Not all units that are available are included, but the general types that can be purchased are illustrated.

CRUDE NONELECTRONIC EQUIPMENT

Hearing trumpets, megaphones, and speaking tubes have long since been replaced by more modern, electronic, auditory training equipment. The old devices, however, served a useful purpose in their day in providing amplified sound to the hearing-handicapped person. Even now the clinician who lacks auditory training equipment may find a "mailing tube" helpful for funneling sound directly to the ear and perhaps also as a motivating device with very young children.

TAPE RECORDER/PLAYBACK UNITS

Many models of tape recorder/playback units are relatively inexpensive and yet quite suitable for recording and playing back practice materials for auditory training. When materials are played back, they can usually be delivered through earphones or a loudspeaker. Whether or not they are played back through earphones or the loudspeaker depends on whether or not a phone connection can be made with the playback system and if the clinician wants the material sent to the sound field via a loudspeaker or directly to the ears through earphones. Figure 14 shows a hard-of-hearing person working with a clinician who is helping him use a tape recorder during an auditory training session.

To record and play back the speech of the patient, the tape recorder/playback unit is quite adequate. It is excellent also for presenting prerecorded taped materials to the hard-of-hearing person. The principal disadvantage of this type of unit is that it is difficult for the patient to compare his own speech attempts with prerecorded materials unless special modifications of the usual unit are made or an arrangement involving more than one channel is used.

Although the ordinary tape recorder/playback unit can function as an auditory training unit, the clinician should consider other units care-

FIGURE 14. *Clinician and client with tape recorder-playback unit.*

fully before recommending its purchase. If funds are limited and the clinician cannot recommend one unit specifically for auditory training and another for tape recording, it may be best to start with the tape recorder/playback and add specialized auditory training equipment when possible.

PORTABLE AUDITORY TRAINING UNITS

As suggested previously, the auditory training units pictured in this chapter are only a few of many on the market. Figure 15 shows a portable unit equipped with a microphone and one set of dynamic headphones. However, this set can have as many as ten phones attached. Figure 16, another portable set, is an all-transistor binaural unit having three adjustments for each ear: gain, frequency response, and output level. Figure 17, another portable transistorized amplifier, can be coupled to either very light or standard binaural headsets. A carrying case is also provided.

Figure 18 presents useful equipment for auditory training. The small unit, powered by a mercury battery, can be worn in a pocket or clipped to clothing. When using this unit, the hard-of-hearing individual can move around in the room and yet be tuned in on all that is happening. The larger unit pictured and an inexpensive magnetic loop are utilized in making this a highly practical and flexible system. In this arrangement there are no cables or wires that restrict movement.

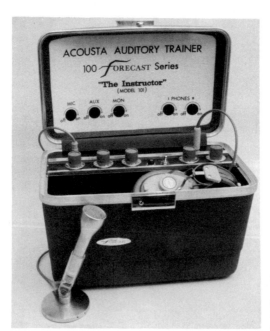

FIGURE 15. *Portable auditory training unit with microphone and headset. (Acousta Auditory Training Units, Albuquerque, New Mexico.)*

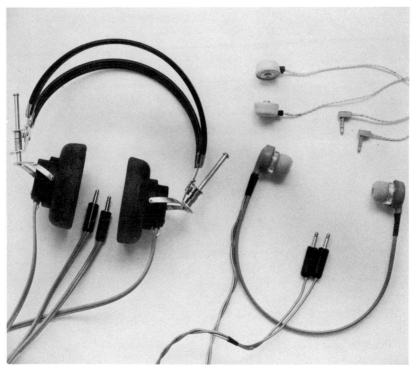

FIGURE 16. *All-transistor portable auditory training unit. (EB Master Auditory Trainer–Model 33, Los Angeles, California.)*

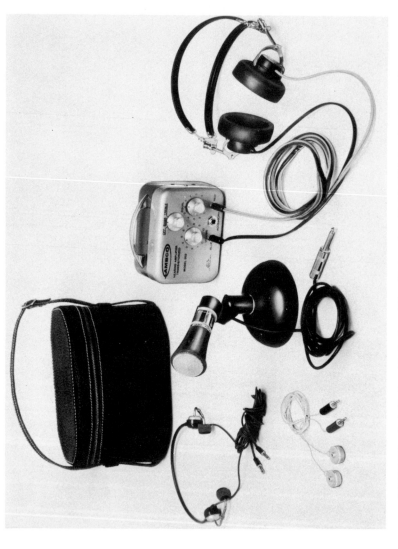

FIGURE 17. Portable transistorized amplifier. (Ambco, Inc., Model 951-B Los Angeles, California.)

FIGURE 18. *A mobile auditory training unit. (Warren Model T-2 Gated Compression Auditory Training Unit—and W-1 Wearable Auditory Training Unit—The Walk Away. Jay L. Warren, Inc., 721 Belmont Ave., Chicago, Illinois.)*

Figure 19 shows a unit frequently used with the hard of hearing in hospitals, educational institutions, and clinics. As the card passes through the playback mechanism, the word, phrase, or sentence on the tape at the bottom of the card is delivered through earphones or loudspeaker. Graded sets of cards can be purchased. Cards can also be purchased that have training material recorded on one track and a second track available for the user to record his own attempts. This arrangement enables a comparison with the model which has just been heard.

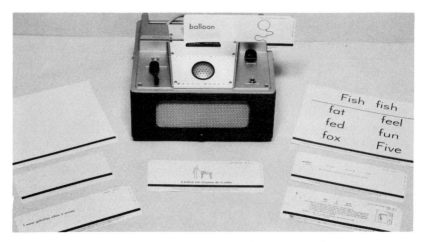

FIGURE 19. *The Language Master. (Bell & Howell, 7100 McCormick Rd., Chicago, Illinois.)*

CONSOLE AUDITORY TRAINING UNITS

In some instances, the console units are considered more desirable than the portable ones. Most of the console models are quite mobile. The set in Figure 20 is complete with a monitor speaker, record player,

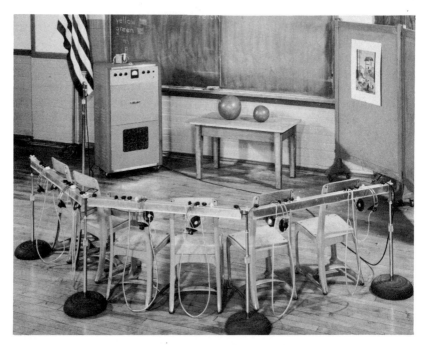

FIGURE 20. *A group hearing aid. (Kenmore Mfg. Co., 903 Maxwell Ave., S. E., Grand Rapids, Michigan.)*

FIGURE 21. *A mobile group auditory training unit. (Acousta—The Administration, Model 602, Broadcast Systems Co., Albuquerque, New Mexico.)*

microphone, and headsets. It can accommodate as many as one hundred receivers. Figure 21 presents a mobile console that can operate up to twenty individually controlled binaural desks equipped with phones and up to twenty microphones. It also contains a recording-playback unit.

CONSIDERATIONS IN SELECTING AUDITORY TRAINING EQUIPMENT

Factors to be considered in the selection of an auditory training unit are: (1) purpose for obtaining a unit, (2) environment in which the unit will be used, (3) type of instruction to be given, (4) funds available for purchasing a unit, (5) guarantee and repair policy, (6) flexibility required, (7) characteristics of the components of the unit, and (8) recommendations of others.

PURPOSE FOR OBTAINING A UNIT

In most instances units will be purchased for use within a clinical setting; however, in some clinics, the units are made available to selected individuals for home use. If a unit will be used in a clinical setting, then all factors should be considered. If, however, the clinician wants a unit for home use, he should select a small, portable, inexpensive unit with a single set of headphones.

ENVIRONMENT IN WHICH THE UNIT WILL BE USED

If the unit is to be used in a classroom for a group of hard-of-hearing students, it must have numerous phone attachments. If the unit is to be used within a hearing clinic, the clinician may or may not wish to select one that has a multiple arrangement.

TYPE OF INSTRUCTION TO BE GIVEN

If the instruction will always be given to groups, the selection will be a group auditory training unit. If the instruction is mainly with individuals, it would be most economical to select a unit designed for individual instruction. The type of materials to be used will also influence selection of a unit for group or individual instruction. If live voice, bells, buzzers, horns, and such devices constitute the majority of the training materials to be used, one can manage successfully without turntables or tape playback components. If tape and/or disc recorded materials are part of the training materials (and they frequently are), then a unit with the necessary components for playing back these materials will undoubtedly be chosen.

FUNDS AVAILABLE FOR PURCHASING A UNIT

Auditory training units vary in price. The smaller, individual sets are less costly, of course, than the more elaborate group units. The clinician should carefully study his needs in relation to available equipment so that he can satisfy his requirements most economically. Great differences in cost exist among models that are highly similar as far as usefulness is concerned.

GUARANTEE AND REPAIR POLICY

The clinician will want to know how the company proposes to guarantee its product. Frequently this is not indicated in brochures advertising the merchandise.

FLEXIBILITY REQUIRED

If one wishes to administer magnetic tape recorded materials, disc recorded materials, or live voice to one or both ears, a flexible unit is necessary. The degree of unit flexibility desired is closely related to the type of instruction that will be given.

CHARACTERISTICS OF THE COMPONENTS OF THE UNIT

A set of specifications is included in almost every brochure describing auditory training units. If no specifications are available, the clinician should request them before ordering the unit. Items such as power and frequency response, power output, and the degree of intermodulation distortion should be known even though auditory training units are not calibrated to fixed reference levels. Assessment of the unit's desirability in respect to its characteristics should include the clinician's demands, based on his knowledge of the response characteristics of the normal ear.

RECOMMENDATIONS OF OTHERS

Although one cannot rely solely on comments made by others about the desirability of a particular auditory training unit, the recommendations of one who has used a unit can often be helpful. If possible, it is desirable for the clinician to talk with a colleague who has purchased and/or used auditory training equipment. One can acquire much information on all types of equipment at the annual convention of the American Speech and Hearing Association, where there are many commercial equipment displays and demonstrations.

SUMMARY

This chapter has focused attention on the equipment available to the clinician involved in auditory training. Basic components of auditory training units were briefly reviewed. Also general types of available auditory training units were described. Emphasis was placed upon the factors to be considered when purchasing an auditory training unit: (1) purpose for obtaining a unit, (2) environment in which the unit will be used, (3) type of instruction to be given, (4) funds available for purchasing a unit, (5) guarantee and repair policy, (6) flexibility required, (7) characteristics of the components of the unit, and (8) recommendations of others.

8

GOOD LISTENING HABITS CONCERN THOSE WHO deal with problems of modern education at all levels, from preschool through adult education. As a result, numerous journal articles and books have been written on the subject. Some writers have dealt with listening as it relates to normal-hearing individuals, whereas others have dealt with the listening problem of the hard of hearing.

This chapter discusses some factors in listening behavior which are relevant to the problems of auditory training for the hearing handicapped: (1) a definition of listening, (2) barriers to good listening, (3) suggestions for improving listening skill, and (4) measurement of listening performance. Some understanding of these four factors

IMPORTANCE OF LISTENING IN AUDITORY TRAINING

should make one aware of the importance of listening in auditory training.

Today, when efforts are being made to facilitate communication in all areas, the topic of listening is receiving considerable attention. Audiologists are certainly not the first to contemplate this topic seriously. The rhetorical theories of Plato and Aristotle show that they considered listening an integral part of oral communication.

A DEFINITION OF LISTENING

For our purposes, listening can be defined as an attitude, a posture, or a mental set that one assumes as he attempts to receive and utilize information transmitted via acoustic events. The term "listening" refers particularly to acoustic events and may be related to the status of one's hearing mechanism at the psychological level. However, the attitude, posture, or set one assumes in listening is very similar to the attitude, posture, or set one assumes in watching. One "cocks his ear" for listening, whereas in watching it might be said that one "cocks his eye." It would be difficult to defend any relationship between listening performance and hearing acuity on a neurophysiological level.

Frequently, someone speaks of "listening ability." Thinking that there is a unitary "ability to listen" would be as absurd as thinking that there is a unitary "ability to learn." As with learning ability, listening ability is probably influenced by numerous factors, such as the listener's motivation, length of presentation of materials, relevance of materials, distracting influences, psychological integrity of the listener, and so forth. Recognition of this fact should not discourage us from attempting to do something about developing good listening performance in cases needing aural rehabilitation, but should motivate inquiry into the complexities of listening behavior. The comparison has been made here between listening and watching. What has been said about these could be said about any of the senses for the attitude, posture, or mental set is the same. We "get set" for reception of stimuli.

The act of listening is learned. In the first few weeks of life, some types of acoustic stimuli cause reflex "startle" reactions and continue to be effective in this respect throughout life. However, early in the child's development, associations are made between acoustic stimuli and certain events that may or may not be pleasurable. Soon the child learns to expect certain things to happen that are related to his auditory experiences. These first associations form the substrata on which more complicated forms of listening behavior develop. If listening is a form of learned behavior, it can be concluded that it is a skill that can be taught. If the skill can be increased through teaching, then there must be some rather logical and systematic approaches to be employed in the training of individuals. Taylor[1] indicates that ". . . in every study reported in which listening instruction had been given, pronounced gains were made in listening and often in allied skills as well."

BARRIERS TO GOOD LISTENING

If listening is an attitude or mental set that causes the individual to "get set" for auditory stimuli, it is reasonable to assume that anything which interferes with this process is a barrier. Ten outstanding barriers are considered here. It becomes the audiologist's responsibility to determine the nature of these barriers for each hard-of-hearing individual with whom he works.

DISTRACTIONS

Distractions that can interfere with good listening are many. The room in which the listening training is taking place can have a distracting effect. Interesting items can compete for the attention of the person in auditory training. Any stimuli that can be received by any of the sensory channels are potential competitors with listening. It might seem farfetched to think that olfactory stimuli could interfere with listening to auditory stimuli until you have tried to carry out auditory training at 11:30 A.M. in a room next to the school cafeteria, from which comes the aroma of meatloaf and gingerbread! Competing auditory distractions can prove troublesome as one attempts to administer auditory training. Blowing horns, slamming doors, and other noises can ruin a therapy session. It is true, however, that as the hard-of-hearing person becomes more skilled in discrimination, distracting stimuli should be included in the lessons.

Visual distractors appear to be equally as potent as auditory ones. Bright lights, moving objects, people, and other disturbances can cause the would-be listener to shift his attention to the visual stimuli and forget his task. It would be interesting and probably useful to construct a series of listening exercises, graded in difficulty with respect to distractors. With this, one could research the effects of various types of distractors on listening performance.

A study by Leonard[2] showed the effects of auditory distractors on

[1] S. E. Taylor, "Listening," *What Research Says to the Teacher,* Research Pamphlet Series, Department of Classroom Teachers, American Educational Research Association of the National Education Association (April, 1964), p. 19.

[2] R. Leonard, "The Effects of Selected Continuous Auditory Distractions on Lipreading Performance" (M.A. Thesis, Department of Speech, Michigan State University, 1962).

lipreading performance. He trained twelve subjects to lipread a filmed speaker saying fifty isolated words. Following training, the test was presented in a "quiet" room with an ambient level of 55 db. In this condition the scores averaged 92.7 per cent correct. The "quiet" condition was followed by one in which white noise was fed into the test room at a level of 80 db at the ears of the subjects. In this condition, lipreading performance of the subjects dropped to 59.7 per cent correct. The third condition was one in which babble was fed into the room at 80 db, measured at the ears of the subjects. Lipreading performance in this condition was 61 per cent correct. The third condition was one in which music was used as the distractor. With music as the distracting agent, the average lipreading score was 62.3 per cent correct. It is interesting to speculate about whether or not the same degree of decrement would be noted in listening scores with visual distractors comparable in relative intensity to the auditory distractors used by Leonard.

INADEQUATE KNOWLEDGE OF RESULTS OF PRACTICE

As pointed out in Chapter 5, it is important to keep the learner fully informed of his successes and failures. When failure occurs, the correct answer and the error response should be indicated. It is not enough merely to inform the hard-of-hearing subject that he has failed. Insufficient knowledge of results of practice can diminish interest in learning and make the would-be listener more vulnerable to distractions.

FEELINGS OF FAILURE

Still another barrier to good listening is a constant feeling of failure in the task. In some instances the feelings may stem from actual knowledge of results of failure; in others, they may be more imagined than real. As the failure experience is compounded, the hard-of-hearing individual becomes more and more demoralized. The only remedy is success.

LACK OF MOTIVATION

The hard-of-hearing person may lack sufficient motivation to become a good listener for one of many reasons. He may really believe that no amount of listening practice can achieve good results—he has a hearing loss and must suffer the handicap that attends it. Those in his immediate surroundings may not encourage him to become a good listener—in fact they might actively oppose his auditory training program. One could speculate at length about factors that cause lack of motivation.

POOR HABITS

Poor habits can hinder becoming a good listener. Nichols and Stevens[3] point out that faking a listening attitude is common and that those who engage in it are only cheating themselves. Another poor habit is not listening closely but merely scanning or attempting to understand generally that which is being presented. Another bad habit is letting the mind wander when close attention is necessary. One can't expect the hard of hearing to make progress in the auditory training session if their thoughts are directed elsewhere. Finally there are those who can be classified, for want of a better term, as lazy. It takes a certain amount of energy to concentrate one's attention on an auditory task. If there is unwillingness to participate actively and remain attentive, little can be accomplished.

EMOTIONAL PROBLEMS

It is not unusual to enroll an acoustically handicapped person who is disturbed emotionally in a program of aural rehabilitation. The degree to which the emotional involvement will affect listening behavior depends on its nature and severity.

One of the writer's clients in an aural rehabilitation program was a young man who suffered a moderate loss of hearing. He was seemingly preoccupied with fear of losing the remainder of his hearing. His attention was extremely poor, he was nervous, he was somewhat incoherent in response, and so on. He was a very poor listener—unable to respond to aural rehabilitation until he received psychiatric help. Following this, he made excellent progress in aural rehabilitation, became an excellent listener, and an active participant in the various aspects of the program.

INAPPROPRIATE MATERIALS

Materials that are too difficult or too simple can hinder good listening. If they are too difficult, they cause despair and if too simple, boredom. There is a natural tendency to stop listening if no success is achieved in the task or if the task offers no challenge.

INTELLIGENCE

It has been suggested that variability in intelligence within normal limits is not as important in listening behavior as was once suspected.

[3] R. G. Nichols and L. A. Stevens, *Are You Listening?* (New York: McGraw-Hill Book Company, 1957), p. 105.

Nichols and Stevens[4] comment that poor listeners are not necessarily stupid people. They found some groups to be better in listening than others. The better listeners did not have as high average I.Q. scores as did the poorer listeners. The poorer listeners were from families whose parents were something other than farmers, whereas the better listeners came from farm families. It would be interesting to determine listening performance as a function of intelligence and measure it in subnormal categories. One might logically assume that the further one explored below normal range, the lower the listening performance scores would be.

LACK OF PRACTICE

Since listening is a skill, it calls for practice by the individual who wants to improve his listening skill. It is not unusual that hearing-handicapped persons are left out of conversations in the home, in social gatherings, or at work. Because they do not participate in conversations, they are deprived of practice in listening. Young children who have been aurally deprived since birth or from early childhood will need special help in learning to listen. They have not used hearing as a primary channel of reception and thus have learned to rely on other sensory input mechanisms.

INADEQUATE UNDERSTANDING OF THE IMPORTANCE OF GOOD LISTENING

Not everyone can be expected to comprehend the importance of good listening. The audiologist must explain to his hard-of-hearing client how he can improve his communication effectiveness by developing habits of good listening. Frequently, this is not easily accomplished. Sometimes it seems that bad listening habits which have persisted over many years are impossible to overcome.

SUGGESTIONS FOR IMPROVING LISTENING SKILL

Numerous suggestions can be made to improve listening. However, regardless of the amount of effort devoted to improving listening skill, the results are sometimes negligible. The suggestions that follow are general and are more successful with some hard-of-hearing persons than with others.

[4] *Ibid.,* p. 11.

PROVIDE AN ENVIRONMENT CONDUCIVE TO GOOD LISTENING

In the practice situation the environment should be relatively free from distracting influences. As the training progresses, it is desirable to make the listening situation more difficult to approximate conditions outside the clinic. The introduction of distracting stimuli should be gradual and carefully planned.

BE A GOOD LISTENER

There is probably no other suggestion of greater importance. Nothing can be so discouraging to a hard-of-hearing person, as trying to talk to one who listens halfheartedly. Incidental learning through the example set by the audiologist is important.

INFORM THE HARD-OF-HEARING INDIVIDUAL OF HIS SUCCESS IN LISTENING TASKS

Immediate knowledge of results is important in training. Trowbridge and Cason[5] exemplified this principle as they measured the effects of informing subjects of their success and failures in a line-drawing experiment. They determined that there was no improvement in a hundred attempts to draw a 3-inch line unless subjects were informed of the success they had achieved.

MAKE SUCCESS POSSIBLE

No one thrives under conditions that produce constant failure. If the hard-of-hearing subject is consistently not achieving, then a critical look should be taken at the methods, materials, situation, and other elements to determine what is causing the failure. Some sense of achievement is necessary so that the audiologist can prevent the hearing-handicapped person from becoming completely discouraged. During each session, the hard-of-hearing person should experience some success in listening performance to sustain his motivation.

PROVIDE REWARDS FOR SUCCESSFUL PERFORMANCE

It is argued that acceptance shown by giving rewards for successful performance creates a situation wherein rejection is implied when performance is not successful. This may be partially true, but it has been

---

[5] M. H. Trowbridge and H. Cason, "An Experimental Study of Thorndike's Theory of Learning," *Journal of General Psychology* (1932), 7:245–58.

this writer's experience that gold stars given to children for successful listening performance can prove to be excellent motivators. The older the handicapped person, the less important it is to provide concrete and tangible rewards. A smile, a word of praise for a successful listening performance is usually sufficient.

DETECT BAD LISTENING HABITS AND HELP THE HANDICAPPED OVERCOME THEM

Early in the program of aural rehabilitation the audiologist should determine if bad listening habits prevail. These should be clearly defined for the aurally handicapped person and countermeasures used to change them. It is sometimes difficult to tell the sweet little old lady of seventy that she is pretending to listen, but somehow the skillful audiologist will manage if this habit obstructs successful listening.

USE APPROPRIATE MATERIALS

The appropriateness of materials is dictated by several factors, the first of which is age. One must not assume that a record of the three bears will interest hard-of-hearing individuals of all ages but must pick and choose the materials to suit each age level. (In Chapter 12 a review is made of various auditory training materials.) Another factor important in selecting materials is the occupation and interest of the adults. Still another is the nature and severity of the hearing loss sustained. One will not encourage those who have sensorineural losses to listen by presenting materials containing tasks of sound discrimination that are too difficult. This is not to imply that such listening exercises should never be given, but that they should be given only when the acoustically handicapped individual is ready for them.

Some materials can be presented regardless of the sex of the hard-of-hearing individual or group. However, if one is to use specialized materials, such as material concerned with tools in the machine shop, items for knitting, and so forth, it as sensible to consider the sex of those with whom these types of materials are used. These are but a few factors to consider in selecting materials to encourage good listening in the auditory training session. The perceptive audiologist will make finer discriminations in selection as he becomes more familiar with his hard-of-hearing clients.

PROVIDE FREQUENT PRACTICE PERIODS

Listening is a skill. Some hard-of-hearing persons will come to aural rehabilitation with much more skill than others. Nevertheless, directed practice will be necessary if improvement is to be achieved. The audiologist will recommend and provide for exercises in listening that are dictated by his evaluation of the need for them. It is important that practice be (1) systematized, (2) made pleasant, (3) be provided according to need, and (4) followed by informing the hard-of-hearing person of his success or failure in the listening task.

EXPLAIN THE PRINCIPLES INVOLVED

Evidence based on classic experiments shows how skills in marksmanship were acquired more rapidly and transferred more successfully when the principles of the tasks were explained.[6,7] Explaining the principles of listening will not guarantee success, but the chances for better listening are improved after such explanation.

The hard-of-hearing person should understand that successful sound perception through listening will vary as a function of (1) the nature of the stimulus—its familiarity and dimensions, (2) the background against which the stimulus is presented, (3) the listener's attitude, which may vary from day to day (4) the potential confusion of the stimuli due to similarity to other stimuli, (5) the amount of practice, (6) the ability to overcome bad listening habits, and (7) the enthusiasm for improving listening skills.

MEASUREMENT OF LISTENING PERFORMANCE

Tests that measure listening are still being developed. However, a few have been completed and made available. These have not been constructed specifically for purposes of aural rehabilitation of the hearing handicapped. One developed by Brown and Carlsen[8] followed a doctoral dissertation focused on the topic of listening.[9] Blewett[10] also dealt with the measurement of listening with students at the college level. Another available test in listening is the graded STEP listening test, published by Educational Testing Service of Princeton, New Jersey.[11] The book by

6 C. H. Judd, "The Relation of Special Intelligence to General Intelligence," *Educational Review* (1908), 36:28–42.

7 G. Hendrickson and W. H. Schroeder, "Transfer of Training to Hit A Submerged Target," *Journal of Educational Psychology* (1941), 32:205–13.

8 *Brown-Carlsen Listening Comprehension Test* (New York: Harcourt, Brace & World, Inc.).

9 J. I. Brown, "The Construction of a Diagnostic Test of Listening Comprehension" (Unpublished Doctoral Dissertation, University of Colorado, 1949).

10 T. T. Blewett, "An Experiment in the Measurement of Listening at the College Level" (Unpublished Doctoral Dissertation, University of Missouri, 1945).

11 *Cooperative Sequential Tests of Educational Progress—Listening* (Princeton, New Jersey: Educational Testing Service, Cooperative Test Division).

Nichols and Stevens[12] is devoted exclusively to the problem of listening and suggests many important factors to consider if one were to try to construct a test of listening.

To gain some information about the listening habits of the aurally handicapped, the audiologist may find it helpful to have an adult client try to scale his own listening behavior. This approach would indicate the individual's appraisal of his listening habits. Such a scale might include the following items.

1. At home I find it difficult to keep listening to conversations that don't pertain specifically to me.
   Always   *Sometimes*   *Never*

2. I find that I listen to men more readily than women.
   Always   *Sometimes*   *Never*

3. I find that I listen to women more readily than men.
   Always   *Sometimes*   *Never*

4. When I'm in a group, I find myself "tuning out."
   Always   *Sometimes*   *Never*

5. When I'm in a situation with loud background noise, I attempt to listen to speech.
   Always   *Sometimes*   *Never*

6. When listening to someone talk for more than five minutes, I find that I let my mind wander.
   Always   *Sometimes*   *Never*

7. If for some reason the person who is talking doesn't appeal to me, I exert less effort to listen to him.
   Always   *Sometimes*   *Never*

8. When I think the listening situation is going to be difficult, I find that I try to avoid it.
   Always   *Sometimes*   *Never*

9. In instances when I am not really listening, I pretend that I am listening.
   Always   *Sometimes*   *Never*

10. I enjoy reading or watching more than listening.
    Always   *Sometimes*   *Never*

The answers to the ten statements above are good indices of the self-evaluation of the hearing-handicapped person's listening behavior. These statements do not include all that is important about listening behavior. Perhaps the reader will want to add to this group.

SUMMARY

This chapter has offered a definition of listening, set forth some of the barriers to good listening, suggested ways to improve listening and meth-

---

[12] R. G. Nichols and L. A. Stevens, *Are You Listening?*, p. 104–12.

ods of achieving a measurement of listening performance. Listening has been defined as a mental set or attitude. It is similar to the attitude one presents as he focuses his attention on or waits with expectation for stimuli to be received by other sensory receptors. The act of listening is learned. Some barriers to good listening are external distractions, inadequate knowledge of results of training in listening, feelings of failure, lack of motivation, poor habits, emotional problems, inappropriate materials, subnormal intelligence, lack of practice, and inadequate understanding of the importance of good listening.

Some suggestions have been made for the audiologist who wishes to help his hard-of-hearing clients improve their listening performance. At the outset it was stressed that an environment conducive to good practice in listening is imperative. Additionally, it was suggested that the audiologist must be a good listener, which is really teaching by personal example. The importance of telling the client the results of his practice attempts was stressed. It was further suggested that success in listening should be made possible during each training period and that proper rewards should accompany success. The importance of detecting a client's bad listening habits was emphasized. It was suggested that careful selection be made of materials for practice in listening, so that they are always the most appropriate ones. Frequency of practice periods was stressed, as was the importance of explaining the principles involved in good listening performance. Finally, some tests were suggested that might prove beneficial to the audiologist who seeks to determine the listening status of those he is training.

9

INDIVIDUAL ATTENTION IS NOT THE ONLY METHOD of dealing with the problems of the hearing handicapped. Auditory training administered in a group situation can help the hard of hearing achieve goals through working with others. Group training has a long and respectable history in institutions where teaching and learning takes place. In schools and various training institutions throughout the country, classes are becoming larger and larger as these institutions attempt to answer the demand of society to educate more and more students. Group work is not peculiar to teaching and learning situations, but has been found useful in psychotherapy.

Group auditory training has some of the char-

GROUP
AUDITORY
TRAINING

acteristics of a teaching-learning classroom situation. Also, it is often similar to the group psychotherapy session. One does not use the group format simply to contact more people in one session, albeit this is a happy byproduct. It is used because of the way in which group structure contributes to success in reaching goals.

THEORETICAL CONSIDERATIONS

Interaction among members of small groups, whose members share equal conditions, promotes sharing of values and norms. The frequent meetings of most auditory training groups, which could be classed as forced-choice groups, create through its members' frequent contact a situation which enables a melding of ideas and values. Berelson and Steiner,[1] in speaking of small groups, suggest that "Shared values include ...such matters as attitudes, tastes, beliefs, and behavioral norms." Thus, it is easy to see the importance of considering group dynamics in working with the hearing handicapped in a group situation.

As one examines the dynamics of the auditory training group structure, he is immediately faced with the concept of relationships. An interpersonal type of relationship exists between clinician and patients and between and among patients. The clinician, in working with the hearing handicapped, strives to create an atmosphere which allows the patients to progress toward their goals. The goals of a single member of the group may be quite similar to those of others in the group for example, (1) better acceptance of his handicap, (2) attainment of better speech, and (3) greater success in group conversation. However, each member of the group has problems that are unique to him as an individual. The clinician must devote individual attention to each member of the group to help each create his goal structure, as it pertains to his own habilitation or rehabilitation. Group auditory training does not stand alone, but depends on individual assistance for its success. The dynamics of individual auditory training are discussed in Chapter 10. The two approaches share common characteristics. Backus[2] suggests that they both consist of a sum of the individuals present, and that psychologically, the interactions among members of the group form a design which is not equal to the sum of the individual members. As for the group structure, this design is determined by the *peer-peer,* plus the *authority figure-peer,* interactions. The alert clinician will create many opportunities for both kinds of inter-

[1] B. Berelson and G. A. Steiner, *Human Behavior* (New York: Harcourt, Brace & World, Inc., 1964), p. 327.

[2] O. Backus, "The Use of a Group Structure in Speech Therapy," *The Journal of Speech and Hearing Disorders* (1952), 17:118.

actions and will utilize particularly the *authority figure-peer* interactions within the group for individual counseling.

BASES FOR GROUPING : A RATIONALE

As previously mentioned, group auditory training is not carried out for the sake of economy. There are some rather well-defined bases for giving individuals the opportunity to work together in a group.

First, a group provides an environment in which the hearing-handicapped individual can feel at ease with others having similar problems. In this environment the handicapped person is freed of the pressures that beset him in less sheltered situations. He has a real sense of belonging to a group and a feeling of increased security. Increased feelings of belonging and security lessen the counterforces which hinder growth within a therapy situation. A group, whose members are in similar circumstances, provides a setting in which anxieties, feelings of guilt, and frustrations can be reduced. Within such a setting the individual can extensionalize, introspect, and through the assistance of the clinician and other members of the group, alter a self-concept that may be preventing proper adjustment to the handicap. Within the group's security, he can seek out meanings of behavior, his and others, that seem to be associated with hearing loss. Thompson,[3] in speaking of the group work with the hearing impaired, states that the successful social experiences of the acoustically handicapped motivate and stimulate the hearing handicapped to want to communicate regardless of their success with oral communication.

The hearing-handicapped individual also spends some time in small groups outside the audiology clinic. Some of these groups are similar to the auditory training group in such respects as size, interests of members, age of members. In these groups the individual frequently experiences the greatest feelings of failure, because he is unable to follow the verbal interchange that occurs. His practice in the auditory training group actually can help him identify reasons for his failure in similar groups outside and suggest methods of preventing failure.

To be successful in working within the group auditory training structure, the clinician must have important qualifications. He must (1) know the dynamics of human behavior, (2) know the dynamics of small groups, (3) understand the psychological ramifications of hearing loss, and (4) be capable of administering therapeutic procedures that will reduce the handicaps associated with hearing loss.

[3] M. L. Thompson, "Group Work with the Hearing Impaired," *Hearing News,* July, 1960.

The second basis for utilizing group structure is that it provides training activities which promote keener observation among the members of the group. It has been suggested[4] that modification of behavior is probably more dependent on sharpening the patient's perceptions than on constant practice of a skill or set of skills.

A third basis for providing group-structured auditory training is the social atmosphere it provides. Frequently the hearing handicapped are unsure of their responses in a social situation because they cannot follow the crosscurrents of conversation. Involvement in a social situation that demands the practice of social skills is very beneficial for the handicapped person because he is also required to compete socially outside the clinic.

Much research has been carried out on the dynamics of small groups. A book edited by Bachrach[5] contains an excellent review of small group research that would be of interest to the clinician involved in group auditory training. Petrullo[6] states that there is considerable theory about the behavior of small groups; however, it is not adequately substantiated by empirical and experimental data.

SOME PRACTICAL CONSIDERATIONS IN PLANNING GROUP AUDITORY TRAINING WITH CHILDREN AND ADULTS

Auditory training for both children and adults has a common goal, which is to train the hard-of-hearing individual to make better use of the remnant of hearing he possesses. In some instances this will involve considerable counseling as well as training; in others, mostly training procedures. The point is that the nature of the training will be determined by the individual needs of those who comprise the group.

A POINT OF VIEW

Auditory training is only one aspect of aural rehabilitation and should be administered along with other rehabilitation measures such as lipreading, speech therapy, speech conservation, and hearing aid orientation. Chapter 11 discusses in detail the need for combining the facets of aural rehabilitation. So that the most meaningful results can accrue from the training, careful assessment must be made of each person's needs before he is placed in the group. As the clinician plans for his auditory training session, he will place differential emphasis on the various aspects of train-

---

4 Backus, *The Journal of Speech and Hearing Disorders*, p. 121.

5 A. J. Bachrach, ed., *Experimental Foundations of Clinical Psychology* (New York: Basic Books, Inc., 1962), pp. 211–53.

6 *Ibid.*, p. 247.

ing, as dictated by needs of those in the group. The training should always be individualized, and this entails thought and planning. At first the task seems impossible to the beginning clinician, but diligent effort, competent guidance, and supervision gradually make it easier.

MOTIVATION

Not all who present themselves as candidates for aural rehabilitation or habilitation are highly motivated. Children come because someone has placed them there. Some adults are literally forced into going to the clinic by some member of the family.

Much can be done to motivate children if the training is fun and exciting. The program can be based on games and other kinds of play activity. In using play as a basis for a clinical session, the beginning clinician sometimes allows the play itself to become the center of focus, and the training becomes second in importance. Never should the clinician or youngster become so enthused with the play activity that the child's success is not evaluated. The progress of the game or play activity should be contingent upon reaching auditory training goals that are set for a particular session.

Although one thinks primarily of play activities for children, the clinician should remember that well-selected game activities can be interesting to adults. The adult should be given sufficient explanation about the objectives, goals, and directions of the training. With this information, the adult can better understand the significance of the training session and thereby cooperate more intelligently.

Whether play activities or an objective explanation of goals is utilized, the hope is to create attitudes on the part of the hearing handicapped that will result in better use of residual hearing. Experimentation shows that competition with self or competition with others can be useful in increasing human learning. The clinician must decide how much competition should be introduced, at what time, and with whom, before creating a competitive atmosphere.

MATERIALS

In Chapter 12 there is a review of auditory training materials that can be used with adults and/or children. The purpose of discussing materials at this point is to suggest some criteria for the selection of materials to be used in group training. Most criteria are the same as one would employ in choosing materials for individual auditory training sessions.

(1) *Appropriate:* (Age) Material selected should be appropriate in several ways. First of all, the clinician should consider the age

range of the group. The writer has seen a session with a well-planned procedure fail because of materials that were either far above or below the ages of the persons to whom they were presented.

(Sex) When selecting material, the sex of the group should also be considered. Of course many materials interest both sexes but uninteresting materials should not be selected. Dolly and her wardrobe generally hold little interest for frog-catching, bug-collecting boys, and vice versa. Materials about the activities at the ladies club would be less than fascinating for most men. However, sex differences are a less important consideration in selecting training materials for adults than for children because adults will usually realize that the material is merely a means to an end.

(Timeliness) An effort should always be made to select materials that are of current interest.

(2) *Attractive:* No argument need be developed for attractiveness as a criterion for the selection of materials. Attractive materials are particularly important when working with children.

(3) *Meaningful:* Clinicians should determine what meaning the material to be used will have for the children or adults involved. The clinician can never hope to know all the potential responses from the persons within the group; nevertheless, some consideration should be given to this criterion. By so doing, the clinician may avoid eliciting some responses that he had not anticipated. With adults particularly, the vocabulary of certain vocations might be extremely meaningful as training material. This would not be the only vocabulary used but might form a valuable central core for training.

(4) *Functional:* Materials to be used with groups should be such that group activity or interaction can be structured around them. Perhaps this entails multiple copies of the material. A game should provide opportunities for all members of the group to participate.

Many materials are available that can be adapted for use with auditory training groups. The development of suitable materials is limited only by the imagination and ingenuity of the clinician. Knowing how, when, and where to use the materials is particularly important. The excellence of materials is only proven by the excellence with which they are employed. Mediocre or poor material in the hands of one clinician might be superior material when used skillfully by another.

Materials serve as aids in the teaching-learning process that takes place in auditory training, and only as aids. The beginning clinician should take some time to construct a few materials that have a general appeal for groups of adults or children. The construction of large amounts of materials, however, can never substitute for knowledge and under-standing of the dynamics that characterize the group of hearing handi-capped with whom he works.

PROCEDURES

The manner in which one proceeds in the administration of group auditory training depends on the needs of the individuals in the group. Some members of the group have so slight a loss of hearing that they do not have a hearing aid, whereas others might wear an aid continuously. Therefore, in the session, the clinician might provide controlled auditory stimulation through a loudspeaker system for those who are wearing aids and those who are not. Other circumstances might involve administering the stimuli through earphones. In other words, three sets of procedural circumstances might prevail:

    (1) Sound field presentation of auditory materials
       (a) to individuals not wearing hearing aids
       (b) to individuals wearing hearing aids.
    (2) Earphone presentation of auditory material.
    (3) Combination of procedures of sound field and earphones to accommodate various needs of persons in the group.

SAMPLE GROUP AUDITORY TRAINING PLANS

For adults.
(1) Major subgoal for this session: Learning to discriminate mono-syllabic words in a background of recorded factory noise.
(2) Hearing loss category of group: Moderate hearing losses ranging from 40–60 decibels average loss for 500, 1000, 2000 cps.
(3) Number of adults in group: Six adults—three men, three women ranging from 35 to 55 years of age.
(4) Number of adults wearing hearing aids: Six.
(5) Setting: Audiology Clinic.
(6) Equipment: Two tape recorders and speaker systems.
(7) Materials: Taped list of 100 monosyllabic words that use vowels [I], [i]; response sheets and pencils; six mimeographed lists of the words; and large score chart.
(8) Procedures:
    (a) Have all aids set at most comfortable loudness levels (MCL) for ordinary conversation.
    (b) Present list of words at an average level of 50 db in quiet—adults listen and write them down.
    (c) Check accuracy with mimeographed lists.

(d)   Place correct scores for each on the large score chart.

(e)   Introduce the factory noise at a level 50 db.

(f)   Present word list in different order once more—adults again listen and write them down.

(g)   Check accuracy with mimeographed lists.

(h)   Place correct scores for each on the large chart.

(i)   Raise noise level to 60 db.

(j)   Present word list in a different order again—adults listen and write them down.

(k)   Check accuracy with mimeographed lists and enter scores on chart.

(l)   Raise noise level to 70 db so that now the signal to noise ratio is 50/70 or −20 db.

(m)   Go through same procedures as before in having adults listen, write, and record scores.

(n)   Compute average scores for each and discuss problems associated with listening in noise.

These procedures can be varied by using different types of interfering noise or music or recorded group conversations, sounds of nature, and others. They can also be varied by keeping the interfering noise constant but altering the sound pressure level of the monosyllabic words.

Procedures similar to those suggested could be used with polysyllables, sentences, and stories. Response to the sentences and stories could be checked through specially prepared tests to determine whether or not the listeners got the messages correctly.

For children.

(1)   Major subgoal for this session: Learning to use visual cues in combination with auditory cues.

(2)   Hearing loss category of group: Moderate hearing losses ranging from 40–60 db average loss for frequencies 500, 1000, 2000 cps.

(3)   Number of children in group: Seven.

(4)   Age level: Primary.

(5)   Number of children wearing hearing aids: Seven.

(6)   Setting: Special room in school.

(7)   Equipment: None.

(8)   Materials: Three colorful cardboard animals (cat, cow, dog) that have been cut into parts like those of a puzzle, and three small boxes for each child containing the parts of the cat, the cow, and the dog. A table set before the group contains three exact drawings of each animal.

(9)   Procedures:

(a)   Be sure all hearing aids are turned on and are set at the most comfortable loudness levels.

(b) Clinician proceeds as follows:
[Jimmy], put a [leg] on the cat. (Words inside the *brackets* are said without voice. They must be lipread if they are to be understood.) Will you please put the head on the [cow], [Leo]?, and so on.

(c) Proceed until all parts of the drawings have been overlaid with the full set of body parts.

(d) The clinician can then use the same technique in getting body parts removed as follows: [Elsie] please give me the [head] of the [dog], or [Charlie], please give [Pat] the [tail] of the [cow].

(e) If the clinician wishes, he may count the number of correct responses and reward those children who have performed best with a star or in some other way,

The plan suggested above could be varied in many ways. Numbers could be substituted for body parts of animals, or an action scene could be substituted for the drawings of the animals. Children could make the requests instead of the clinician.

SUMMARY

Throughout this chapter the theoretical and practical considerations of auditory training in groups have been discussed. It has been emphasized that in group auditory training there is also individualized attention. Prerequisites for clinician success in conducting group auditory training have been enumerated. Problems of motivation by the members of the auditory training group have been discussed, along with the types of materials and procedures that are important. Two sample group auditory training lessons have been presented—one for adults and the other for children.

10

BECAUSE SEPARATE CHAPTERS HAVE BEEN DEVOTED to group auditory training and individual auditory training, they might seem to be mutually exclusive ventures. Such is not the case. Considerable *individual* attention should be given the hard-of-hearing members of the auditory training group. Individual and group auditory training represent two rather distinct approaches that can be, and frequently are, utilized in aural rehabilitation.

THEORETICAL CONSIDERATIONS

The relationship in an individual auditory training session is one of patient and clinician. It is a configuration in which the patient is always interacting with an authority figure. A comparison, through experimentation, of the relative values of individual and group therapy would be valuable.

INDIVIDUAL AUDITORY TRAINING

Excellent training can take place on an individual basis, but the adjustment that can occur through interaction with others who have similar problems is missing. Perhaps the biggest difference between individual and group training is related to the psychological dimension of the whole process. Individuals can drill with their clinicians and learn the skills associated with utilizing their residual hearing to better advantage. They can also ventilate their feelings about their handicap, thereby expressing their perceptions of the problems and frustrations they face, and receive support and guidance from their clinician. In an individual situation, they cannot benefit from sharing their frustrations and problems with others who have similar ones, nor can they encourage others who need such support. In the writer's judgment, the hearing-handicapped person receives the best auditory training, in most instances, if he has the advantage of some group exposure, but his training should be primarily on an individual basis.

REASONS FOR ADMINISTERING AUDITORY TRAINING ON AN INDIVIDUAL BASIS

There are four principal reasons for administering auditory training on an individual basis. The reasons are quite different and are not necessarily equal in importance.

(1) *Concentrated individual attention is indicated.* It is important to determine what the indicators are. One indication of the need for individualized help is the severity of the hearing and/or speech problem. Another is the inadequacy of language function. Still another is the need for individualized assistance because of intense adjustment problems. There are times when personalized attention is indicated in auditory training, before the individual is subjected to the competition that characterizes most groups. The sensitive clinician will determine quickly the readiness for group participation of the more severe cases.

(2) *Patient requests individualized attention.* Normally, one assumes that the clinician will choose the format in which a hard-of-hearing person will receive help. However, the clinician should honor a request for individualized help if at all possible. There may be reasons, not readily evident, that prompt it. If, after working with the handicapped person in individualized instruction, the clinician feels that group auditory training should be given, he should indicate this.

(3) *Cases are distributed for training student clinicians.* Approximately

57 per cent[1] of the hearing centers in the United States are located in universities or medical schools and hospitals. Audiologists are trained in these settings. Therefore, it sometimes becomes imperative that the hard-of-hearing patients be distributed in a way that will provide clinical training material for student clinicians. The supervisor must exercise care in handling this training need so that both student clinician and patient derive maximum benefit.

(4) *Scheduling presents problems.* Individual training must often be chosen for a mechanical reason such as scheduling. However, before too many weeks of work within the clinic, the clinician realizes that with working adults and school children, the realities of the situation often influence the time and frequency of the therapy sessions.

ADVANTAGES AND DISADVANTAGES OF INDIVIDUAL AUDITORY TRAINING

Both advantages and disadvantages can be cited for the individualized approach to auditory training. Some of the obvious advantages are as follows:

(1) *More time.* Obviously if only one person is interacting with the clinician, instead of six or seven, there is more time for assistance with individual problems. Depending on the type of practice, greater progress could occur in a shorter time in individual as compared to a group situation.

(2) *Chance for repeated trials in training.* Even though in good group training an attempt is made to individualize, the same amount of time is not available for this as in individual training. In the individual situation the hearing-handicapped person has more opportunity to stop and evaluate his mistakes and then make repeated trials. Even though some of this can be done, the work in the entire group must continue.

(3) *Better situation in which to discuss adjustment problems.* Although the group situation can help an individual perceive himself more realistically, the individual session also has much to offer. For the person just beginning a program of rehabilitation, whose adjustment problems are intense, the individual session enables the kind of clinician-client interaction that would be impossible in a group.

(4) *Greater opportunity to make constant checks on performance and progress.* In the individual auditory training program, the entire focus is on only one person, and a daily check can usually be made

[1] M. Downs, "Hearing Rehabilitation Centers in the United States," *A.M.A. Archives of Otolaryngology* (1961), 73:65–89.

on performance and progress. Thus, the patient always has a measure of his accomplishments, which can be useful in motivating him to progress further.

The disadvantages inherent in individual auditory training are as follows:

(1) *Deprived of peer evaluations of performance.* There is real benefit in the give-and-take among members of the auditory training group as they evaluate the performances of the others. The person receiving only individual therapy misses this completely, except for the clinician's reflections, which, because he is an authority figure, are not like those of peers. The patient in individual training also misses the opportunity of evaluating his peers' performances.

(2) *Deprived of psychological support of peers.* Although the clinician does provide psychological support when needed, a different kind of support comes from those who share the problems that create handicaps. The person who receives auditory training on an individual basis does not interact with other patients, and therefore does not receive the psychological support of peers.

(3) *Deprived of opportunity to compare and contrast his efforts with others' efforts.* The person in the individual auditory training format has only his own efforts to evaluate and compare with his earlier efforts. This is valuable, but he cannot witness the attempts of others, compare them, and compare his own to them. Such a learning experience is unique to group activity.

(4) *Deprived of opportunity to perform socially in a semisheltered practice environment.* The person receiving individualized training is in a sheltered environment—in which he is interacting with the authority figure and is deprived of social interactions with peers. Actually the group situation is like many other small group situations in which the hearing-handicapped person is involved outside the clinic. Coffee parties, and so forth, can actually be worked into a small group situation and provide a realistic setting for small talk. This kind of opportunity is not available in the individual setting.

SAMPLE INDIVIDUAL AUDITORY TRAINING PLANS

For adults.
(1) Major subgoal for this session: Sound discrimination practice without visual cues.
(2) Hearing loss category of individual: 60–75 db for 500, 1000, 2000 cps.

(3) Wearing hearing aid: Yes.
(4) Setting: Audiology clinic.
(5) Equipment: None.
(6) Materials: List of sentences (100).
(7) Procedures:
  (a) Set hearing aid at most comfortable loudness level.
  (b) Clinician explains to patient that he is going to turn his back and read a list of sentences. After each sentence the clinician says a number which stands for a word in the sentence. This is the patient's cue to construct a sentence with the selected word appearing first in the sentence.
  (c) Clinician proceeds: "Tomorrow is Saturday." "Number 3."
  (d) Patient then responds, "Saturday ____ ____ ____."
  (e) Clinician keeps a list of words missed by patient, which form the basis of a smaller drill list. Words called for by the clinician should be those that are frequently confused with other words.

This lesson can be varied in many ways. One can build a list of sentences that deal with specific topics such as sports, food, travel. Perhaps the clinician will restrict all words asked for to monosyllables. The sentences can be given with varying levels of intensity, and so on.

For children.

(1) Major subgoal for this session: Helping the child to become oriented to his first hearing aid.
(2) Age: 10 years.
(3) Hearing loss category of individual: 30–40 db for 500, 1000, 2000 cps.
(4) Hearing Aid: Yes.
(5) Setting: Audiology clinic.
(6) Equipment: Disc playback.
(7) Materials: Disc containing many different sounds, animate and inanimate.
(8) Procedures:
  (a) Clinician explains the hearing aid's various parts and their functions.
  (b) Clinician demonstrates the various controls with the aid positioned in the child's ear.
  (c) Child then manipulates the various controls.
  (d) Clinician then presents the various recorded sounds from the record: dog barking, children singing, airplane taking off, horn blowing, and others. Sounds are presented at an MCL for the clinician, and the youngster adjusts his gain control to MCL for him.

(e) Clinician then increases the intensity for some sounds and the child makes the adjustment for MCL on his aid.

(f) Clinician then discusses with the youngster the importance of making adjustments of his aid when sounds are "too loud" or "too soft."

The plan just outlined could be altered in many ways. For example, the sounds could be played in quiet and later against a background of noise. Words and sentences could be used in place of the animate and inanimate sounds. Variations in this and other auditory training plans are limited only by the clinician's ingenuity and imagination.

CASE PRESENTATIONS AND DISCUSSION

Since every case has unique features and all individual needs must be considered in training, the clinician should describe the needs of the hard-of-hearing individual after the audiological assessment has been made. The clinician then sees a more complete picture of the person with whom he will work rather than a series of disjointed facts and findings.

The following cases are typical of the many hard-of-hearing individuals who present themselves daily to audiology clinics throughout the country. The brief discussions indicate the areas in need of consideration by the clinician.

(1) *Mrs. D.: age 55, housewife.* Mrs. D. has a severe loss of hearing, with an average loss of 65 decibels throughout the speech range in both ears. Her aided speech-reception threshold, as measured by the CID Auditory Test W-1 and W-2, is at 40 decibels. Her aided PB score is 76 per cent. Mrs. D. is active in church circles and is able to lipread well. She has greatest difficulty in auditory discrimination in crowds. She has just been fitted with a new binaural hearing aid that she likes very much and wears constantly.

Mrs. D. is receiving individualized auditory training, which emphasizes discrimination among sounds in words that have similar acoustical characteristics. Training is given against a variety of noise backgrounds. Her correct scores are showing a gradual increase. Frequently the training is presented without visual cues, as she does not need the lipreading practice. Mrs. D. should also receive group training along with her individualized work.

(2) *Sammy: age 5, preschooler.* Sammy suffers only a slight loss of hearing. His average loss is between 30 and 35 decibels for speech without his aid. With his aid, he can understand speech when it is between 10 and 15 decibels. He is an exceptionally bright youngster who has learned language well despite his handicap. He lipreads fairly well. His speech sound development is poor.

The focus of the training in aural habilitation for Sammy is in speech correction. The [s, ʃ, z, ʒ] sounds are fractionated and are receiving attention in drill work and conversational practice. His therapy is structured around play situations. Auditory training is given primarily to develop better speech sound output by this youngster. Since his lipreading performance is only average, all work is reinforced with visual cues.

(3) *Mr. A.: age 29, engineer.* Mr. A. has just had complete otological and audiological evaluations. He sustains a bilateral loss of 20–25 decibels. He frequently misses words spoken to him at work, and his wife has complained that he is preoccupied at times and very irritable at other times. At home, he alternates between hearing well and hearing very little. He turns the television's volume louder than is comfortable for Mrs. A. and the children. He is a poor lipreader.

Mr. A. is working hard at combining auditory and visual cues. It has not been recommended that he purchase an aid because hearing aid evaluation has shown that he does not profit substantially from one. Much of the vocabulary used in his auditory training is vocabulary often used in the engineering firm in which he works. A close check of his hearing level will be maintained—every two to three months. Mrs. A. has been counseled concerning her husband's loss. She has been told the importance of letting Mr. A. see her face when she speaks to him.

(4) *Mr. P.: age 45, teacher.* Mr. P. has just been fitted with a hearing aid that lowers his speech reception level from 50 to 20 decibels. Nevertheless, Mr. P. thinks that hearing aids are for old men and refuses to wear his, except when he cannot be observed wearing it and it is least needed. Students complain that he simply cannot hear questions and comments directed to him and that frequently he continues talking in defense against student inquiries and comments. Mr. P. does a very inadequate job of lipreading.

The approach with Mr. P. will be mainly one of counseling. Mr. P. must learn that he could use the hearing aid successfully if he would wear it. The scores he achieves when wearing it will be vividly presented to him. The first big task is to force him to keep his first therapy appointment. He came to the audiology clinic at the suggestion of his principal. When and if he does start a program, an attempt will be made to teach him to lipread.

(5) *Mary: age 16, student.* Mary has been severely hard of hearing all her life and has worn an aid since age 5. Wearing her aid, she can achieve a speech reception threshold (SRT) of 55 decibels. Likewise, discrimination is poor—65 per cent, as measured by the CID Auditory Test W-22. Because of her handicap, Mary's academic achievement has lagged. She was enrolled in a special class until age 11, when her parents moved to a locality in which the schools made no special provision for hearing-handicapped children. She is now in the eighth grade. Her speech is very poor, and her articulation is characterized by many distortions and substitutions that result in decreased intelligibility. Her use of visual cues in the communication situation is excellent. She does not seem highly motivated and cooperates passively with the clinician.

In Mary's training, increased speech intelligibility is the long-range goal. Thus, concentrated attention is given to her articulatory problems. Although individual work seems to benefit Mary, she should be included in a group of teenagers receiving auditory training.

(6) *Mr. T.: age 70, retired machinist.* Mr. T. worked in a very noisy shop for forty years. His loss is moderate-to-severe. Speech reception is at 50 decibels unaided and 25 decibels aided. Discrimination is at 76 per cent, aided. For many years Mr. T. knew he suffered a loss but did not seek specialized help. He purchased an aid when he was 47, found it unsatisfactory, and soon discarded it. His lipreading ability is very poor. He is apparently in good health and is very active in lodge and church groups. Presently he wears an aid recommended by a reputable audiologist three years ago.

Mr. T. is very eager to participate in the activities with which he is associated and works concientiously in auditory training. Much of the work with Mr. T. centers on increasing his lipreading skills. There has been some improvement, although quite modest. Effort is made to increase his listening performance, as he would much rather talk than listen. Although auditory training gains are minimal, it seems worthwhile to continue providing rehabilitative procedures for Mr. T. He feels they are very profitable.

(7) *Mrs. K.: age 47, housewife.* Mrs. K. has sustained a very slight loss of hearing in one ear for many years. Recently she noticed that she was having difficulty hearing in both ears. Otological inspection was made, and it was found that her loss was not reversible. Subsequent audiological evaluation showed that her loss for speech, as measured in the sound field, was 40 decibels, and her discrimination score 84 per cent for the CID Auditory Test W-22 lists, presented at 20 decibels above speech-reception threshold. Her recently acquired hearing aid lowers the SRT to 15 decibels. Mrs. K.'s lipreading ability is excellent. There are some signs of speech deterioration, as evidenced by the fact that the [s, z, ʃ] sounds are slightly distorted. Mrs. K.'s auditory training is centered on speech conservation and speech sound discrimination.

(8) *Peter: age 3½, preschooler.* Peter's parents observed for a year and a half that he seemed to be hard of hearing. Only recently did they attempt to have an audiological assessment made. Physical findings by the otologist were negative. Thresholds determined through play audiometry show that the loss is in the moderate-to-severe category. The child is alert and relates very well to those about him. He plays meaningfully and appears to be quite happy. An older sister, age 5, plays with him at home as well as a neighbor boy, age 4½. There is good inner language and good communication with others through gestures.

For Peter, determining the best hearing aid is most important. Following this, auditory training will be directed toward language development. He should be given the opportunity to work in a small group in addition to his individualized training sessions.

SUMMARY

In this chapter, there has been a brief discussion of the individual auditory training situation. Reasons have been discussed for providing auditory training on an individual basis. Some advantages and disadvantages of individual auditory training have been listed. Two sample lessons have been presented: one for an adult, the other for a child. Eight cases have been presented that are considered representative of individuals participating in auditory training clinics throughout the country.

Perhaps the best single conclusion that can be made about individualized auditory training is that it can provide a very useful approach to meeting the needs of the aurally handicapped but should, when possible, be combined with group training. Combined individual and group efforts can be very helpful, not only in terms of increased auditory skills, but also in terms of better self-adjustment and social adjustment.

11

EVEN THOUGH AUDITORY TRAINING, LIPREADING, learning to use a hearing aid, and speech therapy are four distinct tasks, they frequently complement each other in helping the hard-of-hearing individual increase his effectiveness in communication. Auditory training or lipreading alone are inadequate approaches to the problem of habilitation or rehabilitation of the acoustically handicapped. However, each of the four methods will not be a major factor in every case because an aid can solve virtually all communication problems for some people. Whether or not the audiologist must administer auditory training, give lipreading, recommend a hearing aid, or provide speech therapy depends on the results of the tests administered.

COMBINING AUDITORY TRAINING WITH LIPREADING, HEARING AIDS, AND SPEECH THERAPY

The point of concern here, however, is that proper evaluation be made of the individual's communicative effectiveness before he is placed in therapy. Tests of pure tone and speech reception will dictate the need for a hearing aid. Discrimination tests will determine the need for auditory training. Tests of speech reception and discrimination with an aid (if the loss warrants having one) or without an aid will indicate the need for lipreading instruction. Speech therapy is required if speech has failed to develop properly or has deteriorated.

Frequently very young children are placed in a habilitative program before all the facts have been gathered concerning their status and needs. Such a "diagnostic therapy" or "observational therapy" program is designed to obtain a more complete profile of hearing and language deficit. In such instances a "shotgun" approach to therapy may be justifiably employed.

With older children and adults, however, the audiologist must attempt to define carefully the status and need of the hard-of-hearing person. The greater the precision in this task, the more specific the treatment can be. To provide the best type of aural habilitation or rehabilitation service, clinical procedures must be based on the most rigorous scientific assessment of status and need.

COMBINING AUDITORY AND VISUAL CUES

As one contemplates a multisensory approach to therapy with the hearing handicapped, it is logical to consider the relationship that exists between the sense modalities. At one time it was thought that each modality of sensibility operated independently of the others. However, neuroanatomical and psychophysical experimentation indicate some degree of relationship among modalities, particularly between vision and hearing. Certainly one would suspect that, despite neuroanatomical evidence of connections among sensory areas of the cortex, learning has been effective as a causal factor in the response which indicates interrelation For example as one hears a bell ring and simultaneously sees it, he establishes a firm associational bond between the acoustic and visual images. If the person later hears the bell the visual image is clear, and vice versa.

Because strong associational bonds can be established between visual and auditory sense modalities, a combined approach of auditory training and lipreading becomes highly desirable. Even though the acoustic component of a spoken word may be distorted to the hard-of-hearing person and the visual component somewhat obscure, the combined stimuli

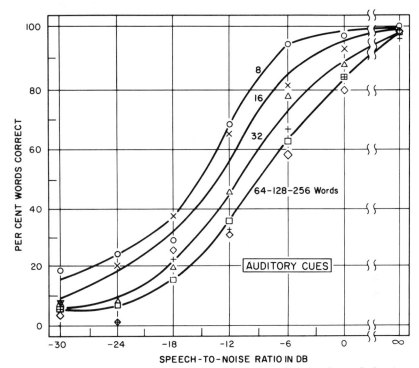

FIGURE 22. *Intelligibility of words presented in noise without visual cues. Each point represents the average results for 450 determinations pooled over subjects.*

provide more cues or information than either one given alone. A third modality to be considered is touch, which is especially important in working with the deaf.

Some laboratory investigations have shown the contribution of the visible aspect of spoken language to speech perception. O'Neill[1] for example, determined that vision contributed 29.5 per cent to vowel recognition, 57 per cent for consonants. As for words, 38.6 per cent of recognition was due to vision and 17.4 per cent for phrases. He further presents visual recognition scores for each of the sounds. Vowels were (O) 76 per cent, (i) 74 per cent, (e) 68 per cent, (u) 64 per cent, (v) 63 per cent, [ɛ] 58 per cent, and (I) 58 per cent. Consonant scores were somewhat higher. They were (s) 86 per cent, (F) 84 per cent, [ʃ] 83 per cent, (P) 80 per cent, (K) 77 per cent, [θ] 75 per cent, and (t) 71 per cent.

Two other investigators showed how vision and audition complement

[1] J. J. O'Neill, "Contributions of the Visual Components of Oral Symbols to Speech Comprehension," *Journal of Speech and Hearing Disorders* (1954), 19: 429–39.

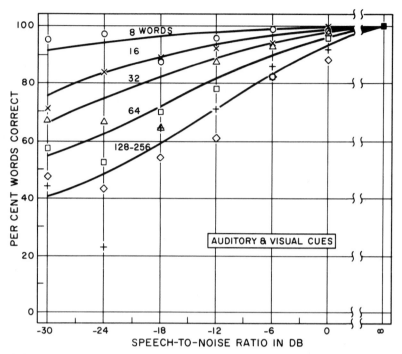

FIGURE 23. *Intelligibility of words presented in noise with both auditory and visual cues. Each point represents the average results for 450 determinations pooled over subjects.*

each other in the task of speech perception. Sumby and Pollack[2] demonstrated that under severe noise conditions 129 subjects who were not formally trained in lipreading performed remarkably better when auditory cues were reinforced by visual cues. Figures 22, 23, and 24 reveal the Sumby and Pollack findings. Figure 22 shows the results of only auditory presentation of the words as a function of speech-to-noise ratio. Note the steady upward swing of the curve as the S/N ratio approaches zero. Figure 23 depicts the success of response in noise as the visual cue is given along with the acoustic. Even at − 30 db S/N, the lowest score was at 40 per cent correct identification. Figure 24 presents a comparison of the data in Figures 22 and 23. This portrayal clearly favors a bisensory approach to training of the acoustically handicapped.

Hudgins'[3] study (similar to that of Pollack and Sumby) of subjects

[2] W. H. Sumby and I. Pollack, "Visual Contribution to Speech Intelligibility in Noise," *Journal of Acoustical Society of America* (1954), 26:212–15.

[3] C. V. Hudgins, "Auditory Training: Its Possibilities and Limitations," The Volta Bureau, Reprint No. 652 (St. Louis: A Keynote Address at the 63rd Summer Meeting, Alexander Graham Bell Association for the Deaf, June, 1954).

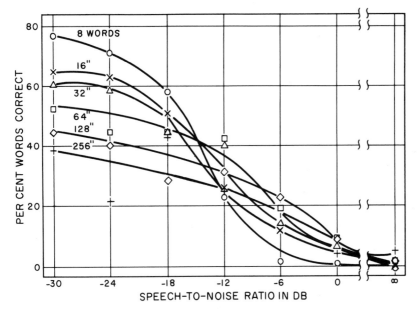

FIGURE 24. *Per cent difference in word intelligibility in noise when auditory and auditory-visual cues are compared. Each point represents the average of 450 determinations pooled over subjects.*

with hearing losses ranging from moderate loss to partially deaf to profoundly deaf showed that speech comprehension was greatly increased by utilizing both auditory and visual cues. Neely[4] also investigated the effects of visual factors on speech intelligibility and found that the addition of visual cues increased the intelligibility of the speech by approximately 20 per cent. Whitehurst[5] summarizes the relationship that exists between lipreading and auditory training when she suggests that "...in one instance the trained eye will fill in the missing auditory links, and in other instances the trained ear will bridge the visual gaps."

HEARING AIDS

The purpose of this discussion is to suggest the importance of the hearing aid in an auditory training program, not to detail the procedures that should be employed in hearing aid selection. For excellent discussion

[4] K. K. Neely, "Effect of Visual Factors on the Intelligibility of Speech," *Journal of the Acoustical Society of America* (1956), 28:1275–77.
[5] M. W. Whitehurst, "Integration of Lipreading, Auditory Training and Hearing Aids," The Volta Bureau, Reprint No. 329, p. 1.

of the topic of selection the reader will wish to check articles by McConnell,[6] McConnell, Silber and McDonald,[7] Miller,[8] Shore, Bilger and Hirsh,[9] Shutts and Resnick,[10] Hardy,[11] and Graham.[12]

It is particularly important that the audiologist clearly indicate to his hearing-handicapped client that the hearing aid is a mechanism which only amplifies sound. This is the single function of the device. It is true that the aid seems to create a whole new world of sound. The world of sound has always been there; however, the hard-of-hearing individual becomes aware of it when it is amplified for him.

The aid cannot improve the physiological function of the defective auditory system. It can enable more successful performance in the auditory aspects of communication, but only because it makes sounds louder to the wearer. Hardy[13] suggests that inappropriate use of the hearing aid at maximum power output might further damage an auditory system characterized by neural impairment.

THE APPROPRIATENESS OF THE AID

Before beginning an aural rehabilitation program, the audiologist should determine whether or not his client needs an aid or if the aid his client is wearing has been selected judiciously. The writer has been confronted by numerous hearing-handicapped persons who were wearing aids that were not lowering their speech-reception thresholds. The audiologist must assess the assistance provided by the client's aid. If the client does not have but seems to need one, the proper evaluations must first be made. Too frequently, speech and hearing therapists working in public schools hesitate to determine an aid's benefit to its wearer. Rather, they assume that it is valuable without taking a critical look.

---

[6] F. McConnell, "The Role of Tests in Hearing Aid Selections," *Hearing News* (March, 1961), pp. 8–9.

[7] F. McConnell, E. Silber, and D. McDonald, "Test-Retest Consistency of Clinical Hearing Aid Tests," *The Journal of Speech and Hearing Disorders* (1960), 25:273–80.

[8] M. Miller, "The Current Status of Clinical Hearing Aid Evaluation," *Audecibel* (1958), 7:6, 8, 17, 18.

[9] I. Shore, R. Bilger, and I. Hirsh, "Hearing Aid Evaluation: Reliability of Repeated Measurements," *The Journal of Speech and Hearing Disorders* (1960), 25:152–70.

[10] R. E. Shutts and D. M. Resnick, "Understanding Your Hearing Aid," *Hearing News* (March, 1959), Vol. 27, 2:3, 4, 5, 12, 13, 14.

[11] W. G. Hardy, "The Hearing Aid: For Whom Does It Work?" *Postgraduate Medicine* (1963), 34:436.

[12] B. Graham, "Hearing Aids: Major Determinates of Their Effectiveness," *Hearing News* (September, 1960), pp. 9–12.

[13] W. G. Hardy, "The Hearing Aid: For Whom Does It Work?"

CONSTANT AMPLIFICATION

In the main, the suggestion that the aid be used constantly during the aural rehabilitation practice periods is excellent. It is argued that the person uses the aid in all kinds of situations outside the clinic, so he should not undergo training without it. However, during the period or periods in which the audiologist is seeking to develop an awareness of the visible aspects of spoken language it is advisable to have the client turn off his aid. If the aid is turned off, the hard-of-hearing person must rely on the visible aspects of speech. By so doing, he becomes aware of additional cues to utilize in the auditory aspect of communication.

SPEECH THERAPY

Since the auditory system is the chief monitor for speech, one would expect that speech output might be adversely affected by malfunction in reception or discrimination of auditory stimuli. Reception and discrimination are affected in proportion to the nature and severity of the hearing loss. The degree to which speech therapy will be employed in aural rehabilitation is determined by the need for it. Some clients, because of the time of onset of their hearing problems, may not need speech therapy. In some cases, the loss is not severe and they have well-established patterns of feedback; however, the audiologist must constantly watch for any subtle deterioration of speech that may occur. In other cases, the observant clinician may detect very slight indications of speech deterioration. The fricatives may be slightly deviant or the (r) and (l) sounds may show signs of deviation. In such cases it is desirable to provide speech therapy designed to prevent further deterioration.

A marked deviation in articulation as well as lack of adequate pitch shift in vocalization are evident in some cases; others show marked deviation in loudness. Individuals who have more severe problems will require immediate and sustained attention to their speech.

Probably the most difficult speech problems encountered in programs of aural rehabilitation are those presented by young children who, because of auditory deprivation, have poorly developed oral language at both receptive and expressive levels. These children require more than the conventional speech therapy approach—they require highly structured therapy in oral language development. The audiologist who tries to combine this type of therapy with auditory training and lipreading must be well versed in the area of language development, the focal point of the other aspects of aural rehabilitation.

SUMMARY

The importance of using a multisensory approach to aural rehabilitation programs has been emphasized. Proper initial assessment of hearing acuity, lipreading performance, and speech of the aurally handicapped person are essential before entering a program of rehabilitation.

The relationship between the sense modalities of hearing and vision has been indicated. Scientific evidence is available that shows the relative contributions of the visual and acoustic components of the code to the perception of language. Such evidence is reason enough to consider only a multisensory approach in training the hard-of-hearing individual.

The appropriateness of a hearing aid and suggestions as to when amplification should be employed have been discussed. It is wise to work without the use of the aid in the early stages of aural rehabilitation to emphasize the value of visible cues.

Speech therapy frequently comprises a part of the program of aural rehabilitation. Young children often need attention in the area of general language development; whereas the approach with adults more often requires remedial work in articulation and some of the vocal attributes such as pitch, loudness, inflection, and so forth. Speech therapy is intimately linked with training in audition and hearing aids, for its success depends heavily on the ear as a monitoring mechanism.

12

MANY MATERIALS ARE AVAILABLE FOR USE IN AUDI-
tory training. Some are recorded on audio discs
and others on the printed page. Unlike many materials available for lipreading training that have
been developed for use with particular methods,
some materials for auditory training have been
developed apart from any particular method or
approach. This has resulted because well-defined
approaches have not developed in auditory training as they have in lipreading. Perhaps the outstanding unique approach to auditory training has
been what some refer to as the "combined approach." Clinicians using this approach seek to
combine auditory training with lipreading and
speech therapy.

REVIEW
OF SELECTED
AUDITORY
TRAINING MATERIALS

As one would expect, some materials are prepared for children and others for adults. This chapter reviews for the clinician selected auditory training materials and their applicability for children and/or adults. The materials included in the discussion represent some of the better materials available. This chapter should acquaint the beginning clinician with materials available for auditory training and stimulate him to develop materials of his own that are best suited to the hard-of-hearing individuals for whom he is responsible.

MATERIALS

RECORDED MATERIALS

Some of the recordings presented here have been made specifically to provide materials for auditory training, whereas others have not.

Mary Whitehurst. Whitehurst narrated a series known as the Hearing Rehabilitation Children's Series.[1] This group of stories is appropriate for early elementary or perhaps preschool youngsters. Many things in each story could provide a basis for questions following the story.

This kind of material is useful in getting youngsters to listen. In addition, she has made available several other records: *Where Is It?* and *Do This; Do That.* These are for nursery school children. The directness and simplicity of the records make them excellent materials for the small child.

Bresnahan and Pronovost. Three records in this series have been constructed specifically as auditory training material for purposes of speech development and reading readiness.[2] These materials consist of sixteen well-graded lessons. The children become involved in tasks of auditory discrimination. The records are constructed as follows:

	Record 1
Side 1–Lesson 1	Words Beginning with B
Lesson 2	Words Ending with B
Lesson 3	Words Beginning with M
Side 2–Lesson 4	Words Ending with M
Lesson 5	Words Beginning with T
Lesson 6	Words Ending with T
	Record 2
Side 3–Lesson 7	Words Beginning with L

---

[1] M. W. Whitehurst, "Tommy's Birthday Present," "The Three Little Pigs," "Hazel Hawkins' Hat," "The Little Dog, Whose Tail Wouldn't Wag." *Hearing Rehabilitation Children's Series* (New York: Gotham Recording Corporation).

[2] M. M. Bresnahan and W. L. Pronovost, *Let's Listen* (Boston: Ginn and Company).

	Lesson 8	Words Beginning with R	
	Lesson 9	Words Beginning with S	
Side 4–Lesson 10		Words Beginning with SH	
	Lesson 11	Words Beginning with ST	
	Lesson 12	Words Beginning with TR	

Record 3

Side 5–Lesson 13		Introducing Rhyming	
	Lesson 14	Rhyming—Words Ending in ING	
Side 6–Lesson 15		Review—Initial Sounds	
	Lesson 16	Rhyming Endings	

The series has been well organized and is accompanied by teaching suggestions for each of the sixteen lessons. There are clearly stated objectives, lesson guides, followup activities, and special notes to the teacher.

Jean Utley. Utley[3] has prepared an auditory training album consisting of two records, which contain many sounds and also stories. They are as follows:

Record 1

Side 1	Chicken	Duke	Tomtom	Horn
	Pig	Sheep	Cowbell	Snapper
	Horse	Dog	Rubber mouse	Doll
	Cat	Goat	Whistle	Bell
	Bird	Cow		Tambourine
Side 2	Train whistle		Gun	Voices:
	Vacuum cleaner		Airplane	Woman
	Telephone		Doorbell	Child
	Tap water		Auto horn	Man
			Piano	
Side 3	Little Boy Blue			
	Jack and Jill			
	Little Jack Horner			
	The Three Bears			
Side 4	The Three Bears (continued)			

The Utley material can be used in a variety of ways—in quiet or against backgrounds of many different kinds of noises. One can use it as test material or as the basis for simple activities.

Arthur and Elaine. The material presented by these two contributors[4] has been designed primarily as practice material for speech correctionists in the form of songs. A manual accompanies the albums, in which suggestions are made concerning the use of the records. Even though the records have been structured primarily for speech improvement and correction, they can aid the clinician giving auditory training to hard-of-

[3] Jean Utley, *What's Its Name?* (Minneapolis, Minnesota: The Maico Co., Maico Building).
[4] Sister Mary Arthur and Sister Mary Elaine, *We Speak Through Music* (Valhalla, New York: Stanbow Productions, Inc., 1959).

hearing children. Each song emphasizes a particular sound of speech. The originators of the material have carefully listed the songs in the order of the genetic development of consonants. Part I presents songs with sounds that children who are three-and-one-half to five-and-one-half years of age are expected to use. Part II has songs that emphasize sounds expected from children five-and-one-half to eight years of age. Sounds that typically are more difficult for children than others, such as [s, l, r], are presented more frequently than are those less difficult to pronounce.

Laila L. Larsen. A familiar album to the rehabilitative audiologists is the one designed by Larsen.[5] It consists of three records: Record 1 is a Consonant Sound Discrimination Test. Records 2 and 3 consist of Consonant Sound Discrimination Drills. These materials are suitable for older children and adults as they require reading skills for their use. In an article appearing in *The Volta Review,*[6] Larsen presents a long list of recorded materials and a word of explanation about their use. The student of auditory training should check this list.

Nora B. Emerson. The Rainbow Rhythms,[7] composed, arranged, and recorded by Emerson, were not specifically designed for auditory training but are meant to be used with children in kindergarten and elementary school. Some basic rhythmic principles such as tempo, accent, and intensity are emphasized throughout the records. The aims of the rhythms are to encourage originality, leadership, poise, alertness, coordination, self-reliance, and perseverance. In all, there are twelve records. A manual of suggested activities accompanies the records. One reason for including these materials is that rhythm is important in speech production. Another reason for their inclusion is that they emphasize listening to auditory stimuli and making appropriate responses to the stimuli.

Ruth Evans. Another fine set of rhythm records was arranged and recorded by Evans.[8] The records are constructed for use by teachers at lower elementary levels. A total of four series are graded to provide a systematic progression of material for the development of rhythmic responses and skills.

Wayne Griffin. A fine collection of sounds to be used in auditory train-

[5] Laila L. Larsen, *Consonant Sound Discrimination* (Bloomington, Indiana: Indiana University, 1950).

[6] Laila L. Larsen, "Recordings for Auditory Training," *The Volta Review* (1951), 51:461–62.

[7] Nora B. Emerson, *Rainbow Rhythms Recordings for Children* (Atlanta, Georgia: Emory University, 1952).

[8] Ruth Evans, *Childhood Rhythms* (Springfield, Mass.: P.O. Branch X, Box 132).

ing are those in the album *Sounds Around Us*.[9] The records are of sounds "Around the House," "Around the Farm," and "Around the Town." Each record is divided into two parts. This set was constructed for use with the Scott, Foresman new basic readers. They provide excellent material for auditory training.

Educational Record Sales.[10] This is a source of auditory recordings that provides graded materials for each level within the public schools. Some of the records that can be useful in auditory training are those that concentrate on instrument recognition, rhythmic play words, and stories.

George W. Frankel. Frankel[11] has constructed three longplay records that present speech materials. They have been designed for hard-of-hearing individuals who do not have the benefit of daily instruction in an audiology clinic. A complete description of the records and plan of training is given by Frankel in *The Eye, Ear, Nose and Throat Monthly*.[12]

PRINTED MATERIALS

The list of materials presented here is not exhaustive and includes materials for both adults and children. Among the materials are some written by persons who have made careers in rehabilitative audiology.

Whitehurst. Whitehurst has contributed a number of meaningful materials for auditory training. Among them are the following:

(1) *Auditory Training Manual*. This book[13] of lessons has been written for hard-of-hearing teenagers and adults. It is so structured that the material can be used in group or individual sessions. Recordings of the lessons are also available. The book is divided into three parts: forty lessons that focus on the sounds of speech; supplementary material, to be used with live voice; and material that stresses recorded speech and music. Whitehurst outlines in detail the procedures to be employed for maximum usage of the materials.

[9] Wayne Griffin, *Sounds Around Us* (New York: Scott, Foresman and Company, 1951).
[10] Phonograph Records and Filmstrips for Classroom and Library—Kindergarten to Grade 12, Catalog 1964. (New York: Educational Record Sales, 157 Chambers Street).
[11] George W. Frankel, M.D., *The Home Auditory Training Program* (Los Angeles, Cal.: distributed by Oto-Sound Laboratories, P.O. Box 49784).
[12] George W. Frankel, M.D., "A Planned Home Auditory Training Program," *The Eye, Ear, Nose and Throat Monthly* (April, 1961), 40:560–62.
[13] Mary W. Whitehurst, *Auditory Training Manual* (New York: Hearing Rehabilitation, 330 East 63rd Street, 1955).

(2) *Let's Travel by Way of Language, Auditory Training, Lipreading, and Speech.* This set of materials[14] is considered by Whitehurst as supplementary material to be used with basic courses in lipreading, auditory training, and speech. The material has been planned for children between twelve to sixteen years of age. Auditory training has been combined with lipreading and speech, and the primary emphasis is on language building. Activities are integrated around a travelogue which takes the hard of hearing to many cities in various parts of the world. There are fourteen units in this book of materials.

(3) *Auditory Training for Children.* This set of materials[15] has been carefully graded and progresses from the simple to that which is quite difficult. The materials have been designed for children between the ages of four and nine. There are seven units of material, each of which is divided into lessons. Whitehurst clearly specifies the aims for each of the units and suggests ways of presenting them.

(4) *Auditory Training for the Deaf.* Even though this material is for the deaf, this book can have some value for the hard of hearing.[16] The authors state that the lessons were primarily designed for those who were deafened before speech was acquired. The book is composed of thirty-eight lessons on the sounds of speech, progressing from the relatively easily distinguished sounds to the more difficult ones. The first five lessons are designed to create habits of critical listening. Lessons six through seventeen deal with the vowels, and lessons eighteen through twenty-one deal with diphthongs. The remaining seventeen lessons are concentrated on the consonant sounds.

(5) *Three Stories to Hear, Color, Read.* This small booklet is simply a coloring book designed for young children that has pictures to be colored and narratives below each picture.[17] There are also recorded materials to be utilized with the three stories.

(6) *Play It by Ear.* This is a collection of auditory training games,[18] compiled as part of a project that received support from the National Institute of Neurological Diseases and Blindness. The chief aim of the manual is to develop good habits of listening among acoustically handicapped children. The manual is primarily intended for parents, although the authors feel that it can be beneficial to teachers of young, hearing-

[14] Mary W. Whitehurst, *Let's Travel by Way of Language, Auditory Training, Lipreading, and Speech* (East Meadow, New York: Hearing Rehabilitation, 1072 North Drive, 1958).

[15] Mary W. Whitehurst, *Auditory Training for Children, A Manual* (East Meadow, New York: Hearing Rehabilitation, 1072 North Drive, 1959).

[16] Mary W. Whitehurst and Edna K. Monsees, *Auditory Training for the Deaf* (Washington, D. C.: The Volta Bureau, 1537 35th Street, N.W., 1952).

[17] Mary W. Whitehurst and Sara W. Thorson, *Three Stories to Hear, Color, Read* (New York: Hearing Rehabilitation, 330 East 63rd Street, 1954).

[18] Edgar L. Lowell and Marguerite Stoner, *Play It by Ear* (Los Angeles: Wolfer Publishing Company, 1960), p. 187.

impaired children. Timely suggestions are made by the authors concerning techniques that may add to the success of playing the auditory training games. Thirty-six activities are presented, and at the beginning of each there is a clearly stated purpose. Instructions are also given as to the materials needed, how to play the game, and variations that can be made. General divisions of this excellent manual are: (1) sounds, (2) music, (3) voice, (4) distance, (5) direction, and (6) an appendix that suggests ways of constructing aids for games, such as flannel boards, paper dolls, doll houses, and other materials.

(7) *Clinician's Handbook for Auditory Training.* This handbook is for children, ten years of age or older, and adults.[19] It is a collection of talker-listener drills to be administered by the trained clinician. The exercises have been graded to provide increasingly difficult tasks in listening, discrimination of speech sounds, and auditory memory span. There are seven units with several lessons in each unit, and suggestions for the teacher preceding each lesson. A unique feature of this handbook is its tear-out pages on which the hearing-handicapped listener may write his responses.

(8) *Tim and His Hearing Aid.* This small booklet can be of real assistance to parents in understanding the hearing aid.[20] The booklet is not a lesson on how to use a hearing aid, but rather a story of the difficulties encountered by a child who needs a hearing aid and of some of the problems involved in making good adjustment to it.

(9) *A Manual for Auditory Training.* There are twenty-four lessons in this manual,[21] and they are divided into two phases of twelve lessons each. In Phase I the emphasis is on discrimination among sounds that vary greatly. In Phase II the stress is on making finer discriminations among sounds that are highly similar acoustically. The main purpose of the manual is to teach hard-of-hearing individuals to make maximum use of residual hearing: by improving the ability to synthesize cues, by increasing memory span, by utilizing intuitive knowledge of situational requirements, and by making optimum use of visual and subliminal cues.

(10) *The ABC of Auditory Training.* The material in this manual is divided into three levels.[22] The first is for ages five to seven, the second for ages six to eight and the third for ages seven to nine. As the lessons progress, they become increasingly difficult. At Level I the adjustment to the group aid is emphasized in preparation for the discrimination tasks

[19] James C. Kelly, *Clinician's Handbook for Auditory Training* (Dubuque, Iowa: Wm. C. Brown Publishers, 1953), p. 155.

[20] Eleanor C. Ronnei and Joan Porter, *Tim and His Hearing Aid* (Washington, D.C.: The Volta Bureau, 1958).

[21] Louis M. DiCarlo, *A Manual for Auditory Training* (Mimeographed).

[22] Sister James L. Hogan, *The ABC of Auditory Training: A Manual for Classroom Use with Young Deaf Children* (St. Louis, Missouri: St. Joseph Institute for the Deaf, 1961), 88 pages.

that follow in the other two levels. The content of the materials is taken from the academic work taught at age levels five to seven, six to eight, and seven to nine. Hogan has attempted to integrate the various facets of aural habilitative procedures, such as lipreading, language development, and auditory training, with speech.

(11) *The New Way to Better Hearing.* This book provides the hard-of-hearing individual with materials that can be used at home.[23] Browd suggests that an "assistant," who can be a layman, should help in presenting the auditory training materials. Lessons are based on the use of speech sounds, sounds other than speech, whispered conversation, face-to-face conversation, and reading materials. Additionally, the book provides information concerning the problems of adjustment that the hearing handicapped must face.

(12) *A Clinical Auditory Training Program.* The writers of this journal article have outlined concisely twenty auditory training lessons for the deafened adult.[24] The purposes indicated by the writers are to improve perception of speech through training with a hearing aid, to increase skills in localizing sounds, to learn the care and operation of a hearing aid, and to increase tolerance for amplified sound. Stress is also placed on improvement of self-adjustment and social adjustment.

(13) *Ways to Better Hearing.* This is another book written for the layman who wishes to help himself to better hearing.[25] It has been structured for the hard-of-hearing adult who is about to select and wear a hearing aid. Brentano outlines a five-step plan for adjustment to a hearing aid by new users. Additional materials are recommended for the reeducation of hearing.

The preceding references cited contain only a few of the many suggestions made by those who have been concerned with the auditory training of the hearing handicapped through the years. As with any other aid in a clinical situation, the recorded and printed material suggested in this chapter are recommended only as aids. They are most effectively used under the guidance of one who understands the problems of the hearing-handicapped child or adult.

SUMMARY

Some of the materials available for auditory training have been described in this chapter. Two categories of materials have been presented:

[23] V. L. Browd, *The New Way to Better Hearing: Through Hearing Reeducation* (New York: Crown Publishers, Inc., 1951).

[24] A. F. Johnson and B. M. Siegenthaler, "A Clinical Auditory Training Program," *The Journal of Speech and Hearing Disorders* (1951), 16:35–39.

[25] L. Brentano, *Ways to Better Hearing* (New York: Franklens Watts, Inc., 1946).

recorded sounds for practice and printed lessons. It has been emphasized that these are but a few of the materials that do exist. The reader should explore more thoroughly the materials mentioned and search for other materials for use. Also it has been suggested that the clinician undertaking auditory training create materials suited to his training environment and to his hard-of-hearing patients.

13

A MULTIPLY HANDICAPPED PERSON IS ONE WHO sustains more than one handicap at a time. The multiple handicap may result from one or more disorders of physical and/or mental function. It must be remembered that handicap and disorder are not synonomous terms. One may sustain a disorder but not really be handicapped by it; on the other hand, a person may be handicapped in several ways because of a single disorder. The measurement of deficit and handicap are not the same.

The multiple handicaps a person may sustain may or may not be related as far as the disorders causing them are concerned. For example, a person might be lame and at the same time hard of hearing. The handicaps resulting from each con-

AUDITORY TRAINING FOR THE MULTIPLY HANDICAPPED

dition would be quite independent of each other as far as the causative factors are concerned. On the other hand, a person might be handicapped from a decrease in both visual and auditory acuity that stemmed from a common neuropathology.

Following is a discussion of some of the disorders and handicapping conditions that are frequently associated with decreased auditory function. Comment is also made concerning procedures to be employed in providing auditory training for the multiply handicapped hard-of-hearing individual.

DISORDERS AND MULTIPLE HANDICAPS ASSOCIATED WITH HEARING LOSS

The following disorders have not been listed with respect to their relative frequency of occurrence or the magnitude of handicapping condition associated with them.

CLEFT PALATE

Children with cleft palates are quite susceptible to middle-ear infections that produce air conduction losses. It is also thought that cleft-palate children can suffer hearing loss because of imbalance in pressures between the middle and outside ear. Insufficient aeration of the middle-ear cavity also can be a factor.[1] There is some difference of opinion concerning the incidence of hearing loss among children with cleft palates. Berry and Eisenson[2] report that less than 60 per cent of the 383 cleft-palate children seen over a nine-year period had hearing handicaps.

The auditory training approach with the hard-of-hearing cleft-palate child will differ very little from that given a hard-of-hearing child who has no problem of cleft palate. However, more time will probably be spent on the habilitative aspects of speech, for the plosives (p-b, t-d, k-g, s-z, ch-j), requiring an extra amount of oral pressure, will probably be distorted. The extent to which speech is affected is directly related to the nature and severity of the cleft. The clinician must make a thorough evaluation of speech adequacy as well as hearing status to deal effectively with this multiple handicap.

[1] Joseph Sataloff and Margaret Fraser, "Hearing Loss in Children with Cleft Palates," *A.M.A. Archives of Otolaryngology* (1952), 55:64.
[2] Mildred Berry and Jon Eisenson, *Speech Disorders* (New York: Appleton-Century-Crofts, 1956), p. 324.

MENTAL RETARDATION

It can be more difficult to carry out a well-planned auditory training program with the hard-of-hearing individual who is mentally retarded than with some others who have multiple handicaps. The reason is that it is often very hard to assess their hearing status accurately. The examiner must determine how much of the communicative inadequacy he observes results from a malfunctioning auditory system, and how much from a lack of mental ability. Several investigators have made systematic attempts to find the best methods of testing the hearing of the mentally retarded. One investigator indicates that estimates of hearing losses among mentally retarded groups vary from 12 per cent to over 50 per cent.[3] Another investigator reports incidence of less than 5 per cent.[4] This figure compares well with the proportion found in normal populations.

Of six auditory tests given to 199 mentally retarded children, Schlanger[5] found that the Speech-Reception Threshold Test proved to be the best choice. He also found that training the subjects substantially elevated their auditory test scores. In a hearing survey of 1220 mentally retarded patients, Rittmanic[6] notes that only a small proportion of the patients can profit from a program of aural rehabilitation. He also noted that impaired hearing can cause behavior that suggests mental retardation.

There seems to be some difficulty in using abstract stimuli, such as pure tones, with the mentally retarded. They seem to respond better to more familiar stimuli such as spoken words, which are more common to them because they hear them more often. Frisina[7] reinforces this notion when he suggest that the intensity of a pure tone must be significantly higher than the normal threshold for the mentally retarded, but when testing with speech materials the higher intensity is unnecessary.

An extensive study was completed at Central Michigan University[8] in

[3] Frank Kodman, "The Incidence of Hearing Loss in Mentally Retarded Children," *American Journal of Mental Deficiency* (1958), 62:675–78.

[4] Chester J. Atkinson, "Perceptive and Response Abilities of Mentally Retarded Children as Measured by Several Auditory Threshold Tests," *Perceptual and Response Abilities of Mentally Retarded Children*, U.S. Office of Education, Co-operative Research Project No. 176 (6471) (Carbondale, Illinois: Southern Illinois University, 1960), pp. 1–47.

[5] Bernard B. Schlanger, "Effects of Listening Training on Auditory Thresholds of Mentally Retarded Children," *ASHA* (1962), 4:273–75.

[6] P. A. Rittmanic, "Hearing Rehabilitation for the Institutionalized Mentally Retarded," *American Journal of Mental Deficiency* (1959), 63:779–83.

[7] D. Robert Frisina, *Basic Considerations in Auditory Training*, Bulletin No. 1, Vol. 9 (Washington, D. C.: Gallaudet College, 1963).

[8] Clarence Webb, Stewart Kinde and Bruce Weber, *Procedures for Evaluating the Hearing of the Mentally Retarded*, Cooperative Research Project No. 1731 (Mt. Pleasant, Michigan: Central Michigan University, 1964), 171 pp.

which 1300 mentally retarded individuals were given auditory tests. The investigators concluded that the concept of "incidence of hearing loss" among populations of mentally retarded has little meaning, except as it is applied to individual studies. They found approximately 25 per cent to be suffering loss of hearing. They further concluded that successful testing of this population was very infrequent when any of their test instruments were used.

Although a multisensory approach is valuable when attempting to nurture more effective communication performance among the hard of hearing, it becomes doubly important that we fully utilize this approach in aural habilitation of the mentally retarded individual. Because of the generally depressed performance in language skills, the clinician should focus directly on this deficit and not become preoccupied with sharpening an [s] sound or attempting to correct a slightly deviant [r]. This type of correction becomes less important in view of the language needs of the hard-of-hearing mentally handicapped person.

Mentally retarded children differ in learning language, depending on the type of mental deficiency that is present. Kirk[9] points out that some brain-damaged children are quite verbal, whereas others have great difficulty in understanding what is said and in expressing themselves. For example the mongoloid is quite deficient in language development. When a hearing deficit is coupled with mental retardation, in which there is such great variability, it becomes difficult, if not impossible, to outline a program of aural habilitation that will apply to all hard-of-hearing mentally retarded children. In planning such a program, a very careful assessment must be made of *each* individual and the work *must* proceed from this point. Furthermore, aural habilitation and rehabilitation must always be conducted under the guidance and supervision of a well-trained clinician.

APHASIA

The child or adult aphasic may sustain a loss of hearing due to malfunction of the peripheral auditory system. When this occurs it only intensifies the clinical problem at hand. The type of aphasia, the severity of central nervous system involvement, and the nature and extent of the loss due to peripheral malfunction will determine the aural habilitative or rehabilitative program. The auditory training to be given will depend on the deficit determined through careful diagnosis. It is very difficult to describe accurately the contribution that peripheral loss makes to the overall picture of the auditory disorder. A good estimate can generally

9 S. A. Kirk, M. B. Karnes and W. D. Kirk, *You and Your Retarded Child* (New York: The Macmillan Company, 1958), p. 104.

be made after careful differential diagnostic procedures have been employed. Auditory training, per se, should be given only after a careful audiological evaluation has been made.

EMOTIONAL DISTURBANCE

Emotional disturbance can occur in the person suffering from hearing problems. The hearing loss can be quite independent of the emotional picture or be a causative factor. The best procedure is for the audiologist to work with other specialists who should be involved, such as the psychologist or psychiatrist. Auditory training will constitute only a part of the therapeutic approach to the problem. Frequently the emotionally disturbed person with a hearing loss comes to the attention of the audiologist before he has any contact with other professional workers. The sensitive, well-prepared clinician will determine in his evaluation the referral sources to be utilized.

CEREBRAL PALSY

It is not uncommon to see hearing loss associated with cerebral palsy. It is frequently observed in the athetoid type of cerebral palsy. In this type there is often a hearing loss in the high frequencies. Westlake and Rutherford[10] suggest that the measurement of hearing level is probably one of the most difficult parts of examining the cerebral palsied. Investigation by Asher[11] shows that there is a far higher incidence of hearing defects among cerebral palsied individuals who have a history of jaundice.

Shere[12] states that in a group of 1293 cerebral-palsied children under comprehensive study hearing defects were found in 7.2 per cent of the spastics, in 18.4 per cent of the ataxics, and 22.6 per cent of the athetoids.

Because of the brain damage that causes cerebral palsy, the clinician frequently observes disturbances in symbolic behavior. Once again, auditory training should be given only after thorough neurological, speech and hearing, and psychological evaluations have been made. The effects of cerebral palsy differ greatly from case to case. As Westlake and Rutherford[13] suggest "Cerebral palsy affects individuals so differently that no

---

[10] Harold Westlake and David Rutherford, *Speech Therapy for the Cerebral Palsied* (Chicago, Ill.: National Society for Crippled Children and Adults, Inc., 1961), p. 14.

[11] Patricia Asher, "A Study of 63 Cases of Athetosis with Special Reference to Hearing Defects," *Archives of Disease in Childhood* (1952), XXVII: 475–77.

[12] Marie O. Shere, "The Cerebral Palsied Child with a Hearing Loss," The Volta Bureau, Reprint No. 750, Washington, D. C.

[13] Westlake and Rutherford, *Speech Therapy for the Cerebral Palsied*, p. 62.

one statement can apply to all of them, and all of the statements can apply to no one of them. Perhaps a few can apply to some of them."

BLINDNESS

It is not unusual to discover hearing deficits among the blind. The aural rehabilitation of the blind precludes the use of a very important approach, lipreading. Thus, the blind with hearing loss present a very difficult clinical problem. Pathways of reception other than the visual should be fully explored as channels through which stimuli can be sent to reinforce those stimuli sent through an impaired auditory system. A monograph published by the American Speech And Hearing Association[14] includes an excellent treatment of auditory rehabilitation of blind persons with hearing impairment.

HANDICAPS ASSOCIATED WITH AGING

Loss of sensory receptor function in individuals who are growing old is not uncommon. The term for hearing loss, as a function of aging, is presbycusis. It may or may not be present with other handicapping conditions. The classic manifestation of this condition of cochlear degeneration is atrophy of the basal coil that results in high-tone deafness.[15] A speech and hearing survey of one of Michigan State University's off-campus clinical operations indicated that approximately 16 per cent of a hospitalized geriatric population showed loss of auditory function. Along with hearing and language malfunction, the following complicating conditions were also noted:

	Per cent			*Per cent*
(1) Cerebral Vascular Accident	44	(8) Diabetic		2.9
(2) Arteriosclerosis	11	(9) Possible Multiple Sclerosis		2.9
(3) Hypertension	5.8	(10) Hip Fracture		2.9
(4) Parkinson's Disease	2.9	(11) Laminectomy		2.9
(5) Brain Damage—Obscess	2.9	(12) Cerebral Degeneration		2.9
(6) Arthritis	8.8	(13) Physical Debilitative		2.9
(7) Osteomyelitis	2.9	(14) Lung Congestion		2.9

Many were fitted with aids. The training of the geriatric group emphasized helping them adjust to their aids and use them most profitably. Those who sustained language disorders as a result of strokes or degenerative neuropathologies were given language therapy, which incorporated

14 "Auditory Rehabilitation for Hearing-Impaired Blind Persons," *American Speech and Hearing Association Monographs* (March, 1965), Number 12.
15 Harold F. Schuknecht, "Presbycusis," *Laryngoscope* (1955), 65:402.

auditory training. Motivation is one of the biggest problems in administering auditory training to a multiply handicapped older person. Although some older people would often rather "tune out" then try to "tune in," many are still "tuned in" regardless of their advancing years.

HEARING LOSS—A MULTIPLE HANDICAP

It is true that several handicaps can stem from a single disorder. Such is the case with hearing loss. When an individual is deprived of auditory input, social and self-adjustment can suffer. A young child may be handicapped in language development and scholastic achievement. Oral language communication is so vital to the development of the whole person that when the input source for information is malfunctioning many areas of development can be affected. An outstanding leader in education for the deaf comments similarly as he points out that deafness involves problems in speech, education, social development, emotional adjustment, and employment.[16] It is, therefore, a multiple handicap.

SUMMARY

Throughout the chapter emphasis has been placed on considerations that must be made as the clinician contemplates administering auditory training to those sustaining multiple handicaps. Generally, the auditory training equipment and materials used with the multiply handicapped are the same as those used with the individual handicapped only in hearing; however, the procedures employed must be designed specifically for each individual. Special consideration was given to those with hearing losses associated with cleft palate, mental retardation, emotional adjustment problems, aphasia, cerebral palsy, and disorders associated with loss of hearing among the geriatric population. Comment was made concerning hearing loss itself as a condition that causes multiple handicaps.

[16] Powrie V. Doctor, "Multiple Handicaps," *Proceedings of the Convention of American Instructors of the Deaf* (Colorado Springs, Colo., 1959), pp. 34–36.

14

THERE ARE SEVERAL REASONS FOR EVALUATING THE effectiveness of auditory training. Probably the most important is to determine the progress in communication skills of any individual or group that received training. This information could be valuable when placing people in a program of aural rehabilitation or recommending dismissal from the program. A second reason for a critical evaluation of training is to determine the effectiveness of a procedure or set of procedures. Results could be useful in planning future training sessions. Certain procedures may work well with some individuals but not with others. Only careful evaluation makes such evidence available. Another reason for careful evaluation of auditory

EVALUATION OF THE EFFECTIVENESS OF AUDITORY TRAINING

training is to learn how individuals are adjusting to their hearing aids.

The evaluation of the effectiveness of auditory training can be relatively informal or formal, depending on the purpose and age of the individual evaluated. The formality of the evaluation procedure usually decreases with age although it is often difficult to make a meaningful formal assessment of very old people.

To evaluate progress that has occurred in a training period, a measurement of certain aspects of performance before and after training is necessary. We must remember that this gives us two measures or sets of measures to compare, and that the training between the first and second assessments is only one series of events in the lives of those being evaluated. The posttraining scores might reflect the training, as well as some other variables that have intervened. To evaluate the effects of practice on human performance is a complex task. When assessing the effects of auditory training, some aspects of performance, such as discrimination or speech intelligibility, might be described by numerical values. However, certain aspects of behavior can be described well in a narrative fashion. These aspects encompass such items as social and self-adjustment of the hearing handicapped and the observed effects of the aural rehabilitation program on these adjustments. As diagnostic procedures are improved, the ability to describe accurately the various kinds of hearing losses is increased. Scientifically based therapeutic approaches are greatly needed for use in programs of aural habilitation and rehabilitation. Previously, we have employed approaches that "seem" to make good sense. One of the *most* neglected areas in the field of clinical audiology is evaluation of the results of habilitation and rehabilitation programs.

Many specific types of evaluations can and should be made by the clinician in charge of auditory training. In most instances the clinician will have reason to evaluate:

(1) Auditory discrimination:
       of environmental nonspeech sounds
       of speech (children's voices as well as voices of male and female adults) of varying types and lengths
       in quiet
       in noises of various types
       with visual cues
       of competing messages
       within specified acoustic bandwidths

(2) Listening.

(3) Speech and language responses:
       intelligibility of speech
       in quiet and noise
       aesthetic evaluation of speech

       language evaluation of children
(4) Localization:
       for sounds in quiet and in various types of noise
           to include common environmental sounds
           to include speech
(5) Adjustment:
       self
       social

AUDITORY DISCRIMINATION

Although the five areas listed are important to the hearing handicapped, discrimination among sounds is probably most vital and most
closely related to the auditory training segment of a program of aural
rehabilitation.

ENVIRONMENTAL NONSPEECH SOUNDS

There are many nonspeech sounds in the environment that are important to us. Some are alerting, such as the doorbell, the cry of the
baby, the stroke of the clock, and so on. Some of them are warning
sounds, such as the siren, police whistle, bark of the dog. And then there
are some sounds, like the chirp of the birds, the neighbor's lawn mower,
rain, and wind, that neither alert nor warn, but simply provide added
information about events around us. There are no well-devised tests to
measure the discrimination for nonspeech sounds. However, the clinician
can easily set up such a set of materials and use them prior to and
following auditory training. A good way to start this might be made
with sound effects records.

SPEECH SOUNDS

The well-known test for discrimination of speech is the C.I.D. Auditory Test W-22. This test, with its many alternate forms, permits one to
derive percentage scores. The lists of words are phonetically balanced
with selected monosyllables. Additionally, the clinician can construct
some materials with children's voices and also voices of female adults that
might aid in evaluating the progress made in auditory training. The
material could be of various types, such as nouns and verbs, and also
of various lengths, namely, monosyllables, polysyllables, short phrases,
and stories.

SOUNDS IN QUIET

It is usually possible to evaluate discrimination in surroundings that are relatively quiet. This provides at least one estimate of the hard-of-hearing person's discrimination performance. Some will show better performance under conditions of quiet than in noise. Environmental nonspeech sounds as well as speech should be used in quiet for the assessment.

NOISES OF VARIOUS TYPES

Since much of the daily activity of humans is carried out against a background of noise, it is wise to determine how well or how poorly the hard-of-hearing trainee discriminates in noise. Again, there is a lack of real test instruments; however, white noise that is available on many clinical speech audiometers provides a good source of controllable noise. If filters are available, selected bandwidths of white noise can be used in testing. This gives the clinician more information about the portions of the sound spectrum that interfere most with the sound discrimination task he is giving the hard-of-hearing person.

SOUNDS WITH VISUAL CUES

Discrimination in backgrounds of quiet and noise is easier with visual cues. In a good program of aural rehabilitation, the auditory training will sometimes be given with visual cues and at other times without. Visual cues from the speaker's face are important, especially in the administration of lipreading tests. A number of lipreading tests have been constructed, although this is an area in which much more work is needed. Several sources will be helpful to the clinician as he seeks to test lipreading.[1, 2, 3]

SOUNDS WITHOUT VISUAL CUES

To measure progress in overall communication effectiveness performance with visual cues must be considered. However, to determine precise-

[1] M. K. Mason, "A Cinematographic Technique for Testing Visual Speech Comprehension," *Journal of Speech Disorders* (1943), 8:271–78.

[2] E. L. Lowell, "A Film Test of Lipreading," *John Tracy Research Papers II* (Los Angeles: John Tracy Clinic, 1957).

[3] H. M. Moser, H. J. Oyer, J. J. O'Neill and H. J. Gardner, *Selection of Stems for Testing Skill in Visual Recognition of One-Syllable Words* (The Ohio State University Development Fund Project Number 5818., 1960).

ly the progress made in auditory discrimination, this skill is measured. Discrimination for speech and the non-speech sounds should be measured without the assistance provided by the visual receptors.

COMPETING MESSAGES

As long as the hard-of-hearing person is required to hear and recognize a sound or series of sounds in the presence of one or more sounds, he is operating under a condition of competing signals. To hear and understand a spoken message uttered in full voice against a background of muffled voices is not usually too difficult. It is much more difficult, however, if two persons are talking simultaneously and both are near the auditor. The auditory discrimination performance of the hard-of-hearing person when subjected to competing messages can be judged by asking him to listen to a message delivered on the left while a different message is delivered simultaneously on the right (or back and front and vice versa). The messages may be taped or delivered by talkers in the sound field.

Another method of testing the ability to discriminate between competing messages is to place earphones on the subject and simultaneously present competing messages in each ear. This approach is not very useful for those who wear hearing aids. If competing messages are used, the clinician will want to use voices of children as well as adults. No definitive test with competing messages has been constructed for the hard of hearing.

SOUNDS WITHIN SPECIFIED ACOUSTIC BANDWIDTHS

If filters are available, speech can be filtered in such a manner that various bandwidths can be presented. For example, one might set the filters to pass only the acoustic energy between 500 cps and 1500 cps or 1000 cps and 2000 cps. By presenting only a part of the spectrum, one makes the task of auditory discrimination more difficult. This is just another method of determining the progress made in discrimination during auditory training. There are, however, no standardized tests of filtered speech designed for the hard of hearing.

LISTENING

To determine what improvement has occurred in listening, the clinician must also appraise this before and after training. The source of one test that has been developed is the Educational Testing Service.[4] Other sources which should be consulted have been cited in Chapter 8. A program of auditory training should not only enhance auditory discrimination performance but also help the hard-of-hearing individual become a more successful listener.

SPEECH AND LANGUAGE RESPONSES

Two principal assessments should be made of speech before and after auditory training. The first concerns the intelligibility of speech. How understandable is the speech? The second one involves an aesthetic appraisal. Are the pitch, rhythm, intensity, and quality components appropriate and pleasant?

INTELLIGIBILITY OF SPEECH

A test of speech intelligibility devised by Black[5] is very useful, especially with high school students and adults. The test with its alternate forms requires reading of word lists and is constructed in such a manner that grading is relatively easy. Intelligibility should be measured in quiet as well as in noise. If no other constant noise source is available, electric fans set into motion will suffice. With children, an informal assessment of intelligibility can be made, in addition to administering such tests as the Bryngelson-Glaspey Speech Improvement Cards,[6] the Templin Articulation Test,[7] the Blanton-Stinchfield Articulation Test,[8] and the Clark Picture Phonetic Inventory.[9]

AESTHETIC EVALUATION OF SPEECH

Perhaps the best way to approach this aspect of the evaluation, which is at best subjective, is with a rating sheet or check list. Aspects such as quality, pitch, and intensity can be rated from poor to excellent along a continuum. Instead of making the rating alone, the clinician should enlist the aid of several other clinicians prior to and following auditory

[4] *Cooperative Sequential Tests of Educational Progress—Listening* (Princeton, N. J.: Cooperative Test Division, Educational Testing Service).

[5] J. W. Black, *Multiple-Choice Intelligibility Test* (Danville, Illinois: The Interstate Printers and Publishers, Inc., 1963).

[6] Chicago, Illinois: Scott, Foresman and Company, 1941.

[7] *Journal of Speech Disorders* (1947), 12:392–96.

[8] Chicago, Illinois: C. H. Stoelting Company.

[9] Denver, Colorado: Communication Foundation, Ltd., Box 8865, University Park Station.

training and thus achieve a combined opinion. This procedure lessens the possibility of too high a rating resulting from the clinicians adaptation to his patient's speech. The test material might consist of single words, sentences, short stories, and spontaneous speech. Again, this is an area in which good test materials should be developed.

LANGUAGE EVALUATION OF CHILDREN

If the clinician wishes to measure language development in the young child, as related to the aural habilitation program, he can gain some information by using lists from the Stanford-Binet (Forms L and M) Intelligence Tests or perhaps the Wechsler for Children (WISC).[10] To measure the vocabulary that is understood by children, the clinician will want to give the Ammons Full-Range Picture Vocabulary Test.[11] A test particularly suited for preschool children is the Smith-Williams Vocabulary Test for Pre-School Children.[12] The Mecham Language Scale[13] is also another means of determining language function among small children.

LOCALIZATION

It is important to know if any progress has been made in teaching the hard-of-hearing person to localize sound more effectively. Because standardized commercial tests are not available, the clinician must develop his own methods of testing whether nonspeech and speech sounds can be localized accurately in space.

ADJUSTMENT

If the clinician is qualified to administer and interpret tests of social and self-adjustment, he should do so before and after the series of group auditory training sessions. If the clinician is not qualified to administer psychological tests but wishes to have this information, he should refer

[10] Psychological Corporation, 304 East 45th Street, New York 17, New York.
[11] R. B. Ammons and H. B. Ammons, *Full-Range Picture Vocabulary Test* (Louisville, Kentucky: Psychological Test Specialists, Station E, Box 1, 1948).
[12] M. E. Smith and H. Williams, *Smith-Williams Vocabulary Test,* University of Iowa Studies in Child Welfare (13), 1937.
[13] M. J. Mecham, *Verbal Language Development Scale* (Philadelphia, Pa.: Educational Test Bureau, Educational Publishers, Inc., 1959).

this part of the work to a qualified examiner. Measures of attitudes, social maturity, and self-concept are important to the clinician. Of course there are means other than formal testing by which the adjustment of the hearing handicapped can be appraised. Among them are field observations.[14] Frequently, the nursery school teacher keeps a cumulative record of the social development of the children, and reports are sometimes available from the principal's office of elementary or secondary schools. Husbands, wives, sons, and daughters can often provide excellent information on the behavior of both children and adults that will help the clinician determine the social and self-adjustment of his patient outside the clinic. Information of this type is sometimes available from employers.

A clinician should make every attempt to measure the effectiveness of his program and thus become better able to serve his patients. Research in all areas of aural rehabilitation, is greatly needed, but particularly in measuring the *effectiveness* of habilitative and rehabilitative procedures.

SUMMARY

This chapter has outlined the specific areas in which testing should occur prior to and following auditory training: (1) auditory discrimination, (2) speech and language responses, (3) listening, (4) localization of sound and (5) social and self-adjustment. Available tests were suggested, and it was emphasized that the clinician must often devise his own evaluation procedures due to the lack of formal testing instruments. Research on methods of assessing progress in auditory training is needed.

[14] A. Anastasi, *Psychological Testing* (New York: The Macmillan Company, 1954), p. 659.

APPENDIX

HOW CLASSROOM TEACHERS CAN HELP
A HARD-OF-HEARING CHILD

(1) Do not overexaggerate when talking to the hard-of-hearing child.
(2) Seat the child in the classroom in such a position that he is not required to look toward the windows when listening to you. Permit him to turn around when others talk.
(3) Do not talk when writing on the blackboard.
(4) In a prolonged discussion of a topic make certain the hard-of-hearing child is following you.
(5) Sometimes names of places and people are difficult for the hard-of-hearing child to grasp. Write these on the board and explain them.
(6) Let the other children in the room be aware of the child's handicap.
(7) Encourage the hard-of-hearing child to participate in extracurricular events.
(8) Be ready to offer special help to the hard-of-hearing child whenever and wherever it is needed.
(9) Become familiar with the parents and homelife of the hard-of-hearing child. By doing so you may greatly assist in effecting carryover of materials you have presented in school.
(10) Encourage a periodic recheck of the child's hearing. If he wears an aid, this too should be periodically rechecked to determine if it is operating properly.

SUGGESTIONS FOR PARENTS OF A HARD-OF-HEARING CHILD

(1) When speaking to the child avoid using a loud voice. Lip movements should not be exaggerated, and the speaker's face should be visible to the child.
(2) When the child is listening to his programs on radio or television, permit him to have the volume at his most comfortable listening level.
(3) Be sure the child has been given a medical examination by a qualified otologist and a hearing evaluation by an audiologist. These two examinations give information about the physical condition of the ears and the level of hearing.
(4) Parents should not purchase a hearing aid unless it has been recommended by an otologist or audiologist.
(5) If the child is in school, parents should keep well informed of his progress by visiting his teacher.
(6) Parents should not attempt to hide the fact that their child is handicapped.
(7) It is wise for parents to provide for periodic checks of their child's hearing and if he wears an aid, of his aid.
(8) Where demands for hearing are made at home, make sure the room is well lighted.
(9) Sometimes hard-of-hearing children withdraw from social situations. It is important that the hard-of-hearing child is encouraged to play with other children.
(10) Hard-of-hearing children should *not* be indulged because they have hearing handicaps.

SPONDAIC WORDS OF AUDITORY TESTS W-1 AND W-2*

(1) airplane	(10) eardrum	(19) iceberg	(28) railroad
(2) armchair	(11) farewell	(20) inkwell	(29) schoolboy
(3) baseball	(12) grandson	(21) mousetrap	(30) sidewalk
(4) birthday	(13) greyhound	(22) mushroom	(31) stairway
(5) cowboy	(14) hardware	(23) northwest	(32) sunset
(6) daybreak	(15) headlight	(24) oatmeal	(33) toothbrush
(7) doormat	(16) horseshoe	(25) padlock	(34) whitewash
(8) drawbridge	(17) hotdog	(26) pancake	(35) woodwork
(9) duckpond	(18) hothouse	(27) playground	(36) workshop

These tests may be purchased from: Technisonic Studios, Inc., 1201 South Brentwood Boulevard, Richmond Heights, Missouri.

CID AUDITORY TEST W-22*

PB-50—LIST 1

(1) ace	(12) deaf	(21) it	(30) or (oar)	(40) thing
(2) ache	(13) earn	(22) jam	(31) owl	(41) toe
(3) an	(urn)	(23) knees	(32) poor	(42) true
(4) as	(14) east	(24) law	(33) ran	(43) twins
(5) bathe	(15) felt	(25) low	(34) see (sea)	(44) yard
(6) bells	(16) give	(26) me	(35) she	(45) up
(7) carve	(17) high	(27) mew	(36) skin	(46) us
(8) chew	(18) him	(28) none	(37) stove	(47) wet
(9) could	(19) hunt	(nun)	(38) them	(48) what
(10) dad	(20) isle	(29) not	(39) there	(49) wire
(11) day	(aisle)	(knot)	(their)	(50) you (ewe)

PB-50—LIST 2

(1) ail (ale)	(12) ease	(25) live	(35) rooms	(46) way
(2) air (heir)	(13) eat	(verb)	(36) send	(weigh)
(3) and	(14) else	(26) move	(37) show	(47) well
(4) bin	(15) flat	(27) new	(38) smart	(48) with
(been)	(16) gave	(knew)	(39) star	(49) yore
(5) by (buy)	(17) ham	(28) now	(40) tare	(your)
(6) cap	(18) hit	(29) oak	(tear)	(50) young
(7) cars	(19) hurt	(30) odd	(41) that	
(8) chest	(20) ice	(31) off	(42) then	
(9) die	(21) ill	(32) one	(43) thin	
(dye)	(22) jaw	(won)	(44) too	
(10) does	(23) key	(33) own	(two, to)	
(11) dumb	(24) knee	(34) pew	(45) tree	

* I. J. Hirsh, H. Davis, S. R. Silverman, E. G. Reynolds, E. Eldert, and R. W. Benson, "Development of Materials for Speech Audiometry," *The Journal of Speech and Hearing Disorders* (1952), 17:321–27.

PB-50—LIST 3

(1) add (ad)	(11) done	(21) is	(31) out	(42) though
(2) aim	(dun)	(22) jar	(32) owes	(43) three
(3) are	(12) dull	(23) king	(33) pie	(44) tie
(4) ate	(13) ears	(24) knit	(34) raw	(45) use
(eight)	(14) end	(25) lie (lye)	(35) say	(yews)
(5) bill	(15) farm	(26) may	(36) shove	(46) we
(6) book	(16) glove	(27) nest	(37) smooth	(47) west
(7) camp	(17) hand	(28) no	(38) start	(48) when
(8) chair	(18) have	(know)	(39) tan	(49) wool
(9) cute	(19) he	(29) oil	(40) ten	(50) year
(10) do	(20) if	(30) on	(41) this	

PB-50—LIST 4

(1) aid	(12) cook	(23) jump	(33) pale	(44) where
(2) all (awl)	(13) darn	(24) leave	(pail)	(45) who
(3) am	(14) dolls	(25) men	(34) save	(46) why
(4) arm	(15) dust	(26) my	(35) shoe	(47) will
(5) art	(16) ear	(27) near	(36) so (sew)	(48) wood
(6) at	(17) eyes	(28) net	(37) stiff	(would)
(7) bee (be)	(ayes)	(29) nuts	(38) tea (tee)	(49) yes
(8) bread	(18) few	(30) of	(39) than	(50) yet
(bred)	(19) go	(31) ought	(40) they	
(9) can	(20) hang	(aught)	(41) through	
(10) chin	(21) his	(32) our	(42) tin	
(11) clothes	(22) in (inn)	(hour)	(43) toy	

These tests may be purchased from: Technisonic Studios, Inc., 1201 South Brentwood Boulevard, Richmond Heights, Missouri.

FIRST AID FOR HEARING AIDS*

SYMPTOMS	READ PARAGRAPHS
Hearing aid dead:	1, 2, 3, 4, 5, 9
Working, but weak:	1, 2, 3, 4, 5, 6, 7, 8, 9, 12
Works intermittently:	3, 4, 5, 9
Whistles:	6, 8, 10, 11
Sounds noisy, raspy, shrill:	3, 4, 5, 8, 10, 11
Sounds hollow or mushy:	1, 2, 7

CAUSES, TESTS, AND REMEDIES

1. *Cause:* Dead or rundown battery. *Test:* Substitute new battery. *Remedy:* Replace wornout battery.
2. *Cause:* Battery reversed in holder so that + end is where − end should be. *Test:* Examine. *Remedy:* Insert battery correctly.

* Reprinted by permission of Sonotone Corporation, Elmsford, New York. Copyright 1959.

3. *Cause:* Poor contacts at cord receptacle of battery holder due to dirty pins or springs. *Test:* With hearing aid turned on, wiggle plugs in receptacles and withdraw and reinsert each plug and the battery. *Remedy:* Rub accessible contacts briskly with lead-pencil eraser, then wipe with clean cloth moistened with dry cleaning liquid. Inaccessible contacts usually can be cleaned with a broomstraw dipped in cleaning fluid.

4. *Cause:* Internal break or near-break inside receiver cord. *Test:* While listening, flex all parts of cords by running figures along entire length and wiggle cords at terminals. Intermittent or raspy sounds indicate broken wires. *Remedy:* Replace cords with new ones. Worn ones cannot be repaired satisfactorily.

5. *Cause:* Plugs not fully or firmly inserted in receptacles. *Test:* While listening, withdraw and firmly reinsert each plug in turn. *Remedy:* Insert correctly.

6. *Cause:* Eartip not properly seated in ear. *Test:* With the fingers, press the receiver firmly into the ear and twist back and forth slightly to make sure that the eartip is properly positioned. *Remedy:* Position correctly.

7. *Cause:* Eartip plugged with wax, or with drop of water from cleaning. *Test:* Examine eartip visually and blow through it to determine whether passage is open. *Remedy:* Disconnect eartip from receiver, then wash eartip in lukewarm water and soap, using pipe cleaner or long-bristle brush to reach down into the canal. Rinse with clear water and dry. A dry pipe cleaner may be used to dry out the canal, or blowing through the canal will remove surplus water.

8. *Cause:* Insufficient pressure of bone receiver on mastoid. *Test:* While listening, press the bone receiver more tightly against the head with the fingers. *Remedy:* Bend the receiver headband to provide greater pressure. This is preferably done by your Hearing Aid Consultant, as he is more skilled in maintaining conformation with the head.

9. *Cause:* Battery leakage (resulting in poor battery connections). *Test:* Examine battery and battery holder for evidence of leakage or corrosion. *Remedy:* Discard the battery and wipe the holder terminals carefully with cloth dampened (not wet) in warm water.

10. *Cause:* Receiver close to wall or other sound-reflecting surfaces. *Test:* Examine. *Remedy:* Avoid sitting with the fitted side of the head near a wall or other surface. Such surfaces tend to reflect the sound from the receiver so that it is more readily picked up by the microphone, thus causing whistling.

11. *Cause:* Microphone worn too close to receiver. *Test:* Try moving instrument to provide wider separation between it and the receiver. *Remedy:* Avoid wearing microphone and receiver on same side of body, or close together.

12. *Cause:* Plastic tubing not firmly seated at hearing aid or eartip ends, or tubing so sharply bent as to block the passage of sound through it. *Test:* Examine and check for tightness at ends. *Remedy:* Push tubing ends firmly onto nubs. See that there is no kink or sharp bend. Replace the tubing if necessary.

INDEX

A

The ABC of Auditory Training, 123-24

Ablation studies, in sound perception, 30-31

Academy of Sciences, Paris, 9

Acoustic bandwidths, 137

Acoustic Method, of M. Goldstein, 10

Acoustic Method (text), 52

Age factor:
  in hearing loss, 20-21, 131-32
  in listening, 87
  in training, 5, 48-49

Aging, handicaps associated with, 131-32

Alexander Graham Bell Association for the Deaf, 54

Alexander of Tralles, 9

American Academy of Ophthal-mology and Otolaryngology, 10

American Speech and Hearing Association, 79, 131

Ammons Full-Range Picture Vocabulary Test, 139

Amplifying devices, electronic, 10-11 (*see also* Equipment)

Anderman, 11

Aphasia, 129-30

Archigenes, 8

Aristotle, 81

Arthur, M., 119

Asher, P., 130

Auditory cortex, in perception, 31

Auditory discrimination performance tests, 17-18

Auditory training (*see* Training)